gestured form and activated space

matthew thomas schlueb

A thesis

submitted in partial fulfillment

of the requirements for

the degree of Master of Architecture

School of Architecture

Pratt Institute

1994

gestured form and activated space

matthew thomas schlueb

Received and approved:

_____   Date: 1/10/95

Chairman and Major Advisor: Richard Scherr

_____   Date: 1/10/95

Dean: Samuel Desanto

SCHLUEBarchitecture Publications
Copyright © 1994

ISBN: 152 399 00 66
EAN-13: 978 152 399 00 61
Second Printing
344
605

Text and images by
Matthew Schlueb

bodies whisper secrets only she can hear

needing her, she listens

falling leaves appear to her as slow motion rain

(subconscious envelopment)

TABLE OF CONTENTS:

ACKNOWLEDGMENTS:

A great many people have contributed to this research project. To begin, much of the development and understanding in the body of this study is a result of the invaluable guidance from the professors at Pratt: Graduate Chairman Richard Scherr, Undergraduate Chairman Deborah Gans, Theoharis David, John Johansen, Giuliano Fiorenzoli, James Rossant, Brent Porter, John Lobell, Martin Skalski, William Fogler, Bill Fasolino, Donald Cromley, and Ann Koll. The professors on this list span the fields of: Architecture, Industrial Design, Art and Design, and Foundation Art.

In addition, much gratitude and debt is owed to the many employees at Pratt who donated time and resources to the construction of the thesis-work installation: President Schutte, Anthony Gelber, Terry Dodge, Van in the loading dock, Skip with the truck, Victor and Tony in the metal shop, Jerry in the wood shop, Eleanor with Schaffer Gallery, and Traci who kept watch over the installation. A special thanks to my roommate Joe, who welded the joints on the steel armature of the thesis-work installation.

Much thanks and appreciation to the many fellow students and friends (far too many to name them all), for their countless hours of discussion and debate over the hypotheses and theories contained within this document. Without their help, this study would have never taken the form and conclusion it has reached.

A never-ending respect and praise to my family and friends in the Midwest, for their continual support and encouragement. Without such a foundation, the countless hours and midnight oil would have never endured. A special thanks to those who had the strength and willingness to review and proofread this material, improving and clarifying the arguments presented: Thomas Schlueb my father, Michael Giuliani, Timothy Allwein, and Brian Lutz to name a couple of the more determined.

And most importantly, my warmest thankyou to the sounding block and backbone of my entire thesis education, my best friend Julianne. Her daily reassurance and belief in the work and the future has been a true inspiration.

(On a footnote: The MetroNorth Rail Road, running into Connecticut, provided hundreds of hours of escape from the stresses and urgencies of the big apple's pace; while also guaranteeing time to read the volumes of research put into this study, during my daily three and a half hour commute.)

ABSTRACT:

Far higher than the material is the spiritual;

far higher than function, material and technique,

stands form.

These three aspects might be impeccably handled

but - if form were not - we would still be living

in a merely brutish world.

So there remains before us an aim,

a much greater and more important task:

to awaken once more an understanding

of form, and the renewal of

architectonic sensibilities.

(Hermann Muthesius)

Here with in, is a desire to explore a hidden dimension of perception: subconscious proxemics in form. Here with in, however, is only a description of form, through semiotics in conceptual space; since a true representation of proxemic relationships is only accessible through somatics in physical space.

This document records the development of an architectural premise beginning with early research in 'form-space' studies, which were then applied to a scale model study of an interstitial / residual space (Main Building's entry hall, on the Pratt Campus), and resulted in a real-scale intervention of the designed gestured forms into the existing campus space. The 'form-space' studies were comprised of gestured forms adjusted through subtle movements, influencing and activating their related spaces. These movements would vary envelopment characteristics of the defined spaces, creating improved conditions in perceptual awareness of spatial thresholds and sensitivity to relational gestured forms. The thesis study's architectural premise was grounded in an attempt to understand the refinement of gestured forms and activated spaces, in addition to an introductory exploration in the proxemics of body and form in architectural space.

The perceived threshold, envelopment, and proxemic qualities of the selected campus space (Main Building's entry hall), were transparent or sometimes near invisible in their existing condition; because of the space's concentrated size and functional-program overload, the displacement of the occupant's perceptions, and a spatial detachment resulting from the occupant's behavioral patterns. In order to define an envelope of activated space and to expose the proxemics within this space, the study was narrowed to a single, particular pattern of movement behavior: 'the sedimentation of occupants waiting for the elevator arrival, amidst the hustle of occupants passing through this sequential space'. This pattern was isolated and adjusted through subtle movements of the installed gestured forms, to find out if proxemics of body and form 'affects' spatial perceptions, human senses, or ultimately behavioral patterns.

The results of this thesis study did find a significant degree of proxemic influence of form and spatial perception in the movement patterns of the occupants in the Main Building's entry hall. The research revealed the influence 'spatial configuration and delineation' has on human behavior, in addition to an ability to measure the location and extremes of spatial thresholds and envelopes. The study also established that human behavior is influenced by 'form positioning and articulation', enabling an analysis of human subconscious and foreconscious perceptions.

The larger intent of the research and observation was to propose a process for adjustment and refinement of gestured form and activated space; not simply to be a case study documenting measurement and analysis of perceptual, proxemic findings. An understanding of the importance of proxemics in architectural space suggests future studies expanding on this subject. One possible direction includes a reversal of the variables, where the human behavior patterns are studied to generate activated spatial threshold and envelopes, and then the gestured forms are introduced to enhance the existence of those patterns, thresholds, and envelopes.

CHAPTER I: INTRODUCTION

One of the primary needs and desires of any life form is a sense of security in its environment; a security that is derived and potentially satisfied through a longing for contact with other life and architecturally, a contact with form and space. (Ittelson and Proshansky, p.217 App.E; Johnson and Marano p.34 App.E; and Gibson p.123-133 App.E)   Contemporary architecture of the mid and late twentieth century seems to have been influenced or responsive to the artificial mediums of the Electronic Age, leaving the more mechanical and physical senses needing and searching for more.   The 'effects' of theological, social, economic, and more recently political and cultural climates on architecture have masked the necessary 'affects' of physical, sensitized, and somatic form and space on the human body and mind. (Eisenman, The Affects p.44 App.E; Pearson p.68 App.G)   This contemporary architecture contains inherent geometries, topologies, and formal dimensions that inadvertently create inadequacies, rendering contemporary society artificial and detached from the more primary and subtle modes of the subconscious body and mind's structures and devices.   The human condition requires a sense of contact or enveloping, which in contemporary times is left only with a detached sublimation or an artificial connection. (Kuspit, Clement p.50 App.G; Wilson p.66 App.B; Freud p.71 App.A)   In the past, the traditional and classical notions of architectural form and space have received a great deal of critical evaluation and refinement through the hands of time and experience, achieving a much more holistic and completed attention to the human model.   However, a void still exists in these former methods which exposes itself in the degeneration and deformation of its interstitial and residual spaces; a void which lurks in the blurred, dulled, and recessed shadows of the hierarchically dominant forms and spaces.   By the displacement of these lesser spaces, there is a production of static or interference in the 'effectiveness' of these refined forms and spaces; a direct cause and solution to the reality of a human detachment from the physical environment. (Rapoport, History p.303 App.E; Hogarth p.62 App.H; Lobell p.205)   An emphasis on the interstitial and residual spaces, engendered by the implications of the more traditional and classical spaces, will heighten the smoothing affiliations of these secondary spaces thereby strengthening the primary spaces' ability to 'affect' the search for contact and envelopment. (Kipnis, Towards p.46 App.A)   Since these secondary spaces are by definition dependent, they will posses imposed geometries; in addition to the human aesthetics' inherent geometries of critical evaluation and refinement, from which a design process can evolve bearing much resemblance to the natural mutation of evolution's own 'natural selection' process. (Alexander, A Pattern p.926 App.H; Skalski p.102 App.H)   A sensitivity to the physical and somatic qualities of these secondary spaces leads to a 'total awareness' (or 'architectural contact'); based on subtle, subconscious implications of interstitial and residual architectural structures and devices.

To test this hypothesis, the Pratt Campus was studied for 'interstitial' and 'residual' spaces resulting from 'classical' / 'hierarchical' spaces; and then a selection of one campus site (the Main Building entry hall) was made to serve as one possible iteration of this theoretical study process.   The analysis of the Pratt Campus made clear various developments over time of the expanding nature of the building forms and urban spaces, in addition to several attempts to unify the diversified growth into a balanced compositional group of classical spaces, hierarchically arranged.   However, in the process of these historic events and actions, there arose the presence of secondary, unplanned, almost accidental, spaces; i.e. interstitial and residual spaces.   Some of these spaces resulted from a simple neglect of design consideration, in their lack of functionality due to their confining dimensions or impractical orientations and locations to the more primary spaces on campus.   Others were bound by a development over time, through the increasing, elevated focus on adjacent forms and spaces that devalue and detract the attention away from their nearby secondary spaces.   And finally, at a more abstract and conceptual level, some of the secondary spaces became interstitial and residual as a result of human behavioral and usage patterns in or around the adjacent or relational primary spaces, rendering the secondary spaces transparent or sometimes near invisible.

From these three criteria for the development of 'interstitial' and 'residual' secondary spaces, the selection of the Main Building entry hall was made, since it held a little of all three characteristics, but most significantly having an emphasis on the latter. In addition to containing 'interstitial' and 'residual' spaces, the entry hall seemed to be the ideal model in that it is a transitional space, while at times acting as a collective and internalized space. Transitional spaces primarily consist of movement behavior, placing an attention on limited exposure to an environment and immediate reactions in perception. While, in contrast, a more collective and passive spatial type will consist of primarily stationary and reclined behavior, focusing on a longer duration of exposure to the environment and indirect reactions in perception. Therefore, by selecting a space that is first transitional and second collective, the effects of the immediate physical environment and perceived spatial envelopes can be better studied, without eliminating the potential to study longer exposure effects (Hall, Handbook p.21 App.D).

The first criteria of an interstitial and residual space was fulfilled by the entry hall's concentrated size and overload of requirements generated by other programs: handling the pedestrian traffic of six independent doorways and a waiting area for elevator usage, in addition to serving as an information source locating the office directory and campus newspapers. Any unplanned gatherings of socializing passerbys or the occasional tour group will instantly turn the perceived space claustrophobic.

Second, the space becomes devalued by the Romanesque, stone portico on the exterior of the entrance. The adjacent, exterior portico becomes a much more inviting space visually, audibly, and environmentally, through a classically refined condition, producing sensations of tranquil release in the cool, shaded, and secluded atmosphere filled with tactile rich materials of stone and wood. When views of this space are forced upon the interior entry hall through a full height glazing system, the only result possible is the degeneration and deformation of the interior space by the displacement of the occupant's perception, ultimately drawing them outdoors.

Most importantly and the subject of a more interesting nature, is the third criteria, a perceptual detachment as a result of the occupant's behavioral patterns and usage. As far as usage is concerned, the most frequent occurrence is the passing of people from the external street to an internal classroom or office or vise-versa (this accounting for sixty percent of the hall's activity). Because of the existing nature of the interior designed space, compounded by the two above, stated factors, the perceived threshold, enveloping, and proxemic qualities of the entry hall space become nearly invisible to the senses (Canter, Psychology p.37-41 App.B; Hall, Handbook p.19-21 App.B). Even during the remaining fractional activity of waiting in a location or place for the arrival of the elevator, the entire sense of 'place' and sensory experience is essentially lost by the confusion and distraction of passing people or the allure of the scenery and activity outdoors. Behavior and traffic patterns dominate the location and means of waiting for the elevator, and the opportunity for a sequential development from street to classroom or classroom to street is incomplete and lost. Reinforcement of a possible sequential space is lost through the transparent nature of the entry hall's spatial thresholds (Kipnis, Post-Analytic App.A). The space's analytic threshold is physically defined by plaster walls and acoustical drop-ceiling tiles, all painted in the institutional-wide 'Pratt White' pigment; all of these materials creating a generic and desensitized experience adding to the transparent nature of the space. The space's contextual threshold is primarily lacking in any unique qualities or providing for any unique occurrences, thereby leaving a similar condition as the analytic threshold, with only a conceptual model of a 'generic' space having almost no conceptual impression or recollection of the space's threshold condition. And lastly, the space's post-analytic threshold is defined by the various political, cultural, theological climates within the entry hall (Pearson p.70 App.B), however these issues are typically latent to the extent that they are practically unnoticed because of the extremely short periods of time spent by the average occupant passing through the space (in most cases less than a minute, even when waiting on the elevator) or because of the lack of any design feature to accent or call attention to these latent issues (Rapoport, History p.282 App.B).

As a result, all of these factors play into the degeneration and deformation of this entry hall space, in relation to the other more primary and planned spaces; and ultimately into the potential this secondary space has on the 'effective' quality the primary spaces can maintain, and the 'affective' quality the secondary space can produce (Eisenman, The Affects p.43 App.G). By narrowing the study to a single, particular type of movement behavior inherent to the entry hall space; influences from body and form proxemics can illustrate spatial 'affects' on perception and ultimately movement behavior; validated through proxemic measurements (Wilson p.64 App.G). After there is an understanding of these spatial 'affects' occurring within this entry hall's secondary space, adjustments can be made to refine and increase their 'effectiveness' (Alp p.151 App.L); thereby strengthening any existing or new architectural connections, with the occupants of the space.

CHAPTER II: METHODOLOGY

In the design of the gestured forms introduced into the selected site, a focus was placed on the need to define an envelope of activated space (defined by gestured forms), locating the sedimentation of occupants waiting for the elevator arrival, amidst the hustle of the transitional occupants passing through this sequential space.   Four gestured forms ranging in size from a human scale up to a slightly larger than human scale (Fig. 1, 2, and 5 thru 8); were designed to create that perceived envelope of activated space (Heider p.69-78 App.D), adjacent to the elevator door.   An attempt was made to alter the passing occupant's spatial assessment of detached and activated envelopes (Gibson p.100-122 App.B); as they walk by the elevator in a sequence from the exterior portico to the offices or classrooms.   By doing this, the transitional occupants receive an indirect awareness of the 'affective' quality in this site, in addition to the more direct awareness perceived by the occupants waiting on the elevator.   Therefore, by enhancing the interstitial and residual nature of this site through a focus on the sedimentation of occupants adjacent to the elevator door, the space's threshold will be reduced in transparency; while adding to the sequential relationship of the more primary spaces on the exterior and interior of the main building.

Figure 1: Installed Gestured Forms
Above: Detail of materials (wood, steel, and wire) and fabrication process.
Below: Three installed gestured forms (Form-A, Form-B, and Form-C); view from
the President's Office, looking toward the Across Gallery.

Figure 2: Details of Installed Gestured Forms

Figure 3: Independent Study (Paired Study Models)
These paired study models are one example of the design process used to generate the installed gestured forms. The study models are paired together to illustrate the subtle adjustments, refining the gestured forms and activated spaces.

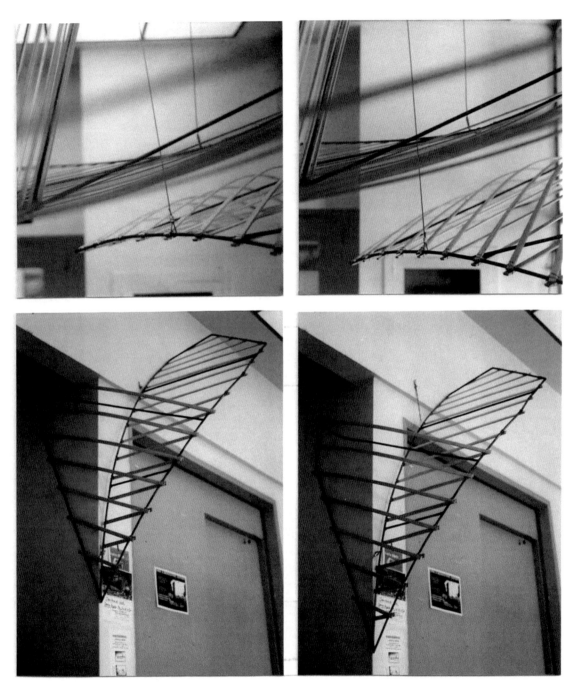

Figure 4: Adjustments to Installed Gestured Forms
Above: Form-C was adjusted six inches from the earlier installed condition, lowering
the projecting pointed edge (oriented toward the elevator).
Below: Form-B was lowered eight inches from the earlier installed condition.

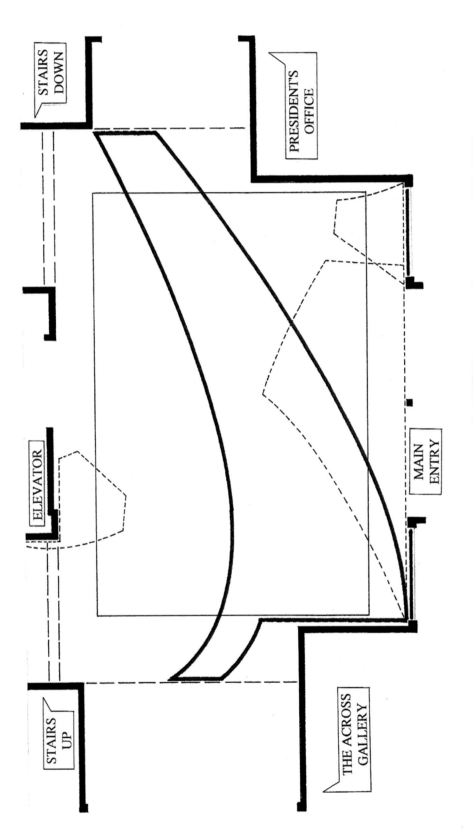

Figure 5: Form-A

Form-A consists of two surfaces, a concave vertical surface and a convex horizontal surface. The concave vertical surface defines an open space in front of the elevator, dividing the entry hall in half: a constricted front half and an open rear half. The convex horizontal surface follows the other surface's curved edge, constricting the front half of the entry hall by defining a new ceiling plane at seven feet off the floor. (For photographs, refer to Fig. 1 and 2)

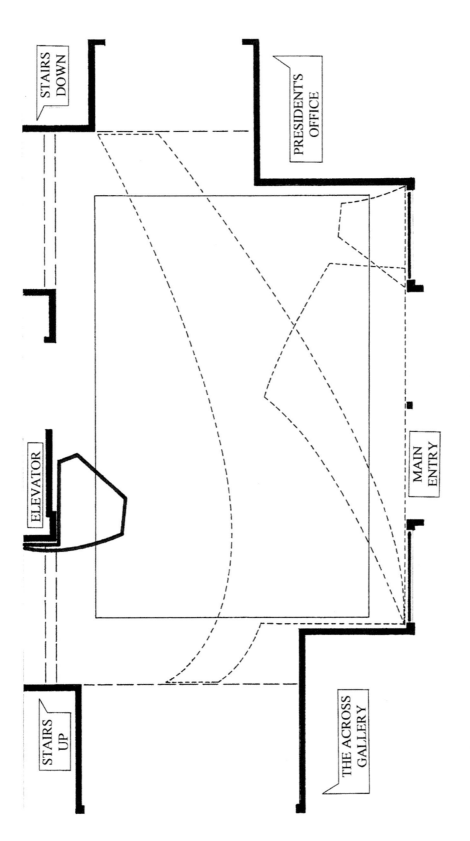

Figure 6: Form-B

Form-B consists of two surfaces, a concave vertical surface and a convex vertical surface. The convex vertical surface wraps the corner as it expands up the staircase, hinting of the gestured forms in the entry hall. The concave vertical surface defines a smaller envelope of space immediately in front of the elevator door. (For photographs, refer to Fig. 1 and 4)

STAIRS DOWN

PRESIDENT'S OFFICE

ELEVATOR

MAIN ENTRY

STAIRS UP

THE ACROSS GALLERY

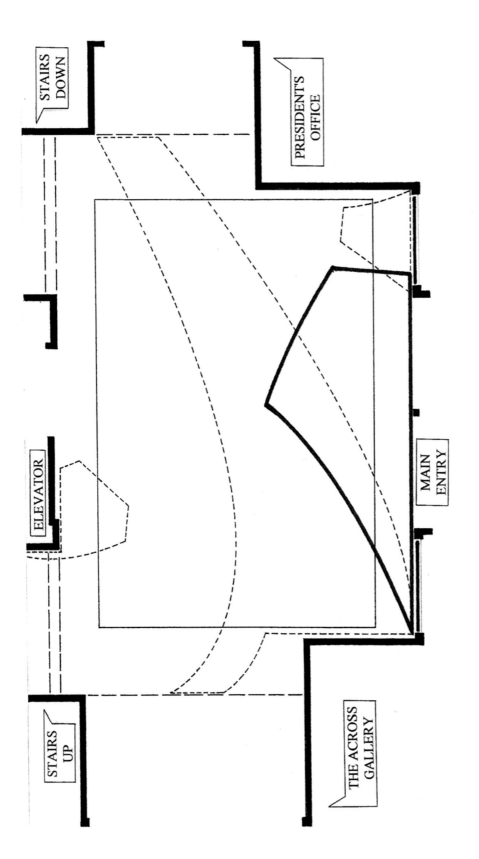

Figure 7: Form-C

Form-C consists of two convex horizontal surfaces. The first of the two surfaces, is oriented toward the floor plane, at seven feet off the floor plane. This surface has an inverted concave bend, defining a spatial envelope at the threshold of the main entry. The second surface follows the inverted bend mirroring the first surface, engaging the horizontal surface of Form-A. (For photographs, refer to Fig. 1, 2 and 4)

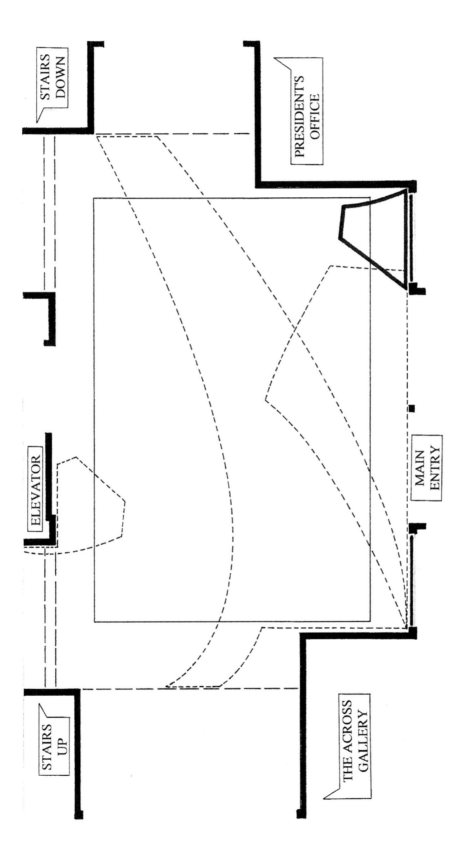

Figure 8: Form-D

Form-D consists of a single folded surface, extending vertically from the floor plane up to a point at six feet off the floor. This dimension gives the form a human scale, engaging the occupants of the entry hall. The fold in the surface creates two concave halves, one defining a lower perimeter to the spatial envelope activated by the lower surface of Form-C. The other half engages the floor plane.

In order to enhance the interstitial and residual quality of this space through a reduction in the threshold's transparency, attention to the vocabulary of the installed forms was necessary. The perceptual awareness of this installation was paramount to the 'effectiveness' of these forms; since any new awareness, perceiving the space's threshold, would heighten any existing minimal awareness. The vocabulary of the installed forms, was made to be more sculptural in materials, fabrication, and spirit, than architectural. However, their 'affectiveness' to manipulate spatial perception and their detailing of connections reacting to the existing site's idiosyncrasies, were the means to an architectural treatment of the site's implications. The form's vocabulary was made sculptural, in order to facilitate a dialogue with the occupants, predominately art faculty and art students. After there was an increase in perceptual awareness, both conscious and subconscious, the adjustment and enhancement of the spatial envelopes and threshold's opacity would then be possible.

The installed form's vocabulary was pivotal in another way, aside from a relation to the occupants using the space. The effects of the space's constricted size and potentially claustrophobic perception, influenced the decisions made in creating a vocabulary that would not contribute to an already severe problem. A transparent nature in the forms was a requirement for any additional surfaces that would be reducing the space even more. The higher the transparency, the less intrusive the forms would become. However, the forms needed to be detected to some degree, or they would be of no use in redefining the existing spatial thresholds and proxemic relationships. In order to find a middle ground between transparent and perceivable, the surfaces were created with a repetition of wooden strips leaving an open space (varying from two inches to six inches) between each strip. This would allow the surface to appear transparent with no perceived threshold of space when viewed at a right angle (within an envelope of space defined by a concave surface) to the surface. It would then take on the character of a solid surface, defining a spatial threshold, when viewed from a skewed angle looking down the length of the surface (Fig. 2). By manipulating the surface in this manner, spatial envelopes could be perceived externally, influencing the occupant; and then disappearing and avoiding claustrophobia once the occupant moves into those envelopes of space (Crick p.36-41 App.B; Crick p.53 App.C; Crick p.206-207 App.C).

The spatial envelopes, to be perceptually enhanced, define and contain specific moving and standing activities organized into behavioral patterns within this selected site. The installed forms frame the envelopes that contain these patterns, rather than describing the patterns directly. This displaces enhancement from the architectural intervention onto the perceptual awareness of the interstitial and residual spaces, while still enhancing the behavioral activities indirectly. The method of framing the space and not the functional activity avoids the problematic assumptions made in the design process related to structuring events and usage reasoning. Enhancement of the defined thresholds in the spatial envelopes brings a new awareness to the site's patterns, ultimately encouraging new desired activities.

The majority of this thesis study involves the adjustment and enhancement of the spaces containing those activities revolving around the elevator doorway. The adjustments to the spatial envelope adjacent to the elevator, were made in a similar manner to the refinement process studied earlier in multiple model studies, during thesis research (Fig. 3, refer to Schlueb, Independent p.2-34 App. M). In that process, gestured forms were adjusted through subtle movements, influencing and activating their related spaces. These movements would vary envelopment characteristics of the defined spaces, creating improved conditions in perceptual awareness of spatial thresholds and sensitivity to relational gestured forms. Figure 4 illustrates two examples of an adjustment made to a gestured form, refining the envelopment characteristics with their related spaces. The refining adjustments of activated spaces made through movements of the installed gestured forms; exposed manipulations of spatial perception and behavioral activities (Craik, The Comprehension p.36 App.B). From a site intervention, a greater understanding was possible beyond the traditional model studies investigated at the architectural studio level (Ittelson and Proshansky p.234 App.L; Collins p.20 App.K); this was made clear with the differences found between the earlier model study (one inch scale) of the selected site and the installation of the designed forms into the actual space (human scale).

The adjustments to the gestured forms could have taken many different directions and resulting effects on the behavioral activities. One possible option of adjusting the installed forms was to add a skin membrane to the ribbed wooden strips. This would increase the perception of the spatial thresholds, enabling the measurement of transparency and opacity influences. Another option was to apply the 'Pratt White' pigment to the wooden strips. This adjustment would transform the installed forms from a sculptural materiality into a structure with surfaces that become camouflaged within the surrounding 'Pratt White' walls. This type of transformation would measure the differences in the impact of an introduced sculptural form in contrast to an invisible objectivity that places emphasis on purely subconscious perception of physical proxemic thresholds. However, even though these two adjustments are related (possibly to be explored later as a further investigation of the entry hall and the installed forms), they are of a different nature study. In this thesis study, as introduced with the research conducted earlier in the independent study (Fig. 3, refer to Schlueb, Independent p.2-34 App. M), the nature of adjustments revolved around the manipulation of the physical form. Several options presented themselves, the first possibility was the removal of an entire gestured form from the context of the other three forms. This would measure the specific affects that the removed form contributed to the installed condition of the entry hall (Barker, Ecological p.16-17 App.I). To focus the study, the positioning of a gestured form could be moved slightly, measuring the changes in spatial envelopes related to the portion moved (Hogarth p.93-94 App.H; Hogarth p.95-107 App.F). This was the method used in the earlier independent study involving the paired study models, and therefore would best illustrate any differences in designing with scale models as opposed to the actual space (this being one of the original reasons for the construction of the gestured forms at a human scale and introduced into the actual entry hall, refer to Collins p.20 App.K). More intensive study could continue, adjusting the forms to a refined condition, through subtle re-scaling or re-forming of the initial forms at critical points in the form's gesture. This would measure the degree of affectiveness a gesture can have on spatial envelopes. The extent of this study was simply to imply the potential for research in the manipulations such as these, by recording a single iteration of the many possible adjustments of gestured forms.

When locating the gestured forms into the entry hall to influence the spatial conditions that existed, there was an issue of physicality that needed to be addressed. The gestured forms could have been installed at the floor level, thereby physically obstructing the movement potential of the entry hall's occupants. This would create a study of the gestured forms, measuring the degree to which movement patterns would shift and structure themselves relative to the installed forms; adjusting the placement of the forms to record these shifts. However, the choice of a conceptual form of perception over a physical perception was selected. This conceptual study was achieved by suspending the gestured forms from the ceiling above the eye level of the occupants, thereby making no physical obstruction to the occupant's movement patterns by their installation. This resulted in a study that could measure the degree to which subconscious perceptions influence movement behaviors within defined spatial envelopes (Crick p.205-210 App.B).

The gestured forms that were introduced into the entry hall were design and refined with the issues described above, developed first in a model format to be followed by a study in the actual entry hall. By retaining a focus on the occupant's behavior related to the space around the elevator door, the installed forms could be created with an attention to the perceptual and spatial issues influencing those behaviors (Heider p.8 App.G).   While the design decisions involving the refinement of the gestured forms can be found in the earlier research done in the independent study (Schlueb, Independent p.2-34 App. M), this chapter will help to establish the context and concepts that were instrumental to the creation and development of the installed forms.

CHAPTER III: OBSERVATIONS

The study and observation of the installed gestured forms in the entry hall was based on and controlled by the dependent variable: 'movement patterns' of the occupants using the entry hall (Winkel and Sasanoff p.352-353 App.J).   By using the movement patterns as a variable dependent on the activation of space resulting from the gestured forms, the observations would be structured to reflect the physical proxemic nature of the occupants; thereby demonstrating a validity to the thesis premise and execution.   Using movement patterns (behavior mapping) avoids the difficulty of asking the occupants to describe the influence the forms have on their perceptions.   Most of the occupants are unaware that any change in their behavior is taking place, since the affects from the gestured forms are primarily at a subconscious level of perception (Ittelson and Proshansky p.218-221 App.L; Ittelson and Proshansky p.232 App. K).   First, the movements of individual occupants are recorded; restricted to the observations made when the entry hall was only occupied by one occupant, to eliminate any proxemic influences from other occupants.   Then, the individual observations are grouped into patterns of similar movements (factor analysis), to reveal recurring behaviors linked to physical characteristics in the entry hall (Ittelson and Proshansky, p.222-224 App. L; Winkel and Sasanoff p.359 App.J).   Any change in their behavior resulting from the adjustments of the forms is visible in these patterns and can be mathematically analyzed and validated to find the form's efficacy in influence over the occupant's behavior.

The observation of these movement patterns requires many controls, to create a study with only one dependent variable. One of these controls is the sample of occupants used in the study. In order to create a natural and unprovoked response to the installed forms, the occupants that were studied needed to be unaware of the study or its intent (Ittelson and Proshansky, p.229 App. G). To facilitate this, in addition to maintaining the same sample of occupants using the space over the duration of the study (including adjustments to the forms), the observations were conducted at the same time and day of each week: Tuesdays and Thursdays, one hour of time samples between 9 a.m. and 11 a.m., one hour of time samples between 1 p.m. and 3 p.m. (Table 1).

Another concern was the degree of the initial 'shock value' in the installation of the gestured forms into the existing space. The observations of the occupants in the existing condition is the result of many weeks, months, and sometimes years of the occupants exposure to the empty entry hall, a behavior that has become repetitive, familiar, and desensitized (Kipnis, Of Objectology p.105 App.A). In order to maintain a similar response after the forms were installed, a period of time allowing for significant exposure to eliminate the initial 'shock value' or 'exploratory' responses was necessary (Stea p.14 App.C; Downs and Stea p.9 App.C; Ittelson and Proshansky p.236-237 App.C). This was done by installing or adjusting the forms for a minimum of eight days before any observations were recorded. In addition, the second group of observations of the 'Installed Condition' was held back for an extra fourteen days, to verify the validity of this premise (Table 1). The results of these observations spread out over a four week period, in contrast to the observations of the 'Adjusted Condition' spread out over a two and a half week period, proved to validate the occurrence of a desensitizing initial response over repeated exposures to the context.

The recording of the movement patterns was done with two forms of visual observation: still pictures and moving pictures. The still pictures were taken with a Nikon FA 35mm camera, using Kodak Plus-X pan 125 asa speed film, and developed on Kodak Polycontrast III RC Lustre paper. The moving pictures were taken with a Quasar CCD Quarter Back palmcorder, using JVC VHS-C 90 min videotape. The entry hall was observed from the portico adjacent to the entry hall (ten feet away from the main entry); taken through the full height glazing system dividing the two spaces. The cameras were positioned to record the movements of the occupant's feet in relation to locational cues given from the tile work inlaid in the floor. In addition, the cameras also recorded the occupant's body orientation (and change in orientation) to the gestured forms, lateral displacement of the occupants, proxemic distances (and change in distances)

Table 1: Observation Schedule

Fall Semester, 1994:

Week 5:	Observed 'Existing Condition': October 4th and 6th 21 time samples, 212 individual paths
Week 6:	Observed 'Existing Condition': October 11th and 13th 25 time samples, 288 individual paths
Week 7:	Installed Gestured Forms into the Main Building Entry Hall October 14th and 17th
Week 8:	Observed 'Installed Condition': October 25th and 27th 22 time samples, 312 individual paths
Week 10:	Observed 'Installed Condition': November 8th and 10th 23 time samples, 320 individual paths
Week 11:	Thesis Presentation: Preliminary Review November 16th and 17th
Week 12:	Adjusted Gestured Forms, to attempt a Refinement November 21st
Week 13:	Observed 'Adjusted Condition': November 29th and December 1st 24 time samples, 276 individual paths
Week 14:	Observed 'Adjusted Condition': December 6th and 8th 23 time samples, 304 individual paths
Week 16:	Thesis Presentation: Final Review December 20th
	Thesis Submitted: January 3rd, 1995

between the occupants and the gestured forms, gestures (degree of movement) of the occupants in relation to the gestured forms, kinesic isomorphism of the occupants in relation to the gestured forms, eye behavior of the occupants in relation to the gestured forms, and the occupant's bodily involvement seeking / avoiding contact with the gestured forms (Hall, Handbook p.57 App. K).   These cues would provide much more information in a study that researched the spatial relationships involved with its occupants; however for this study of limited scope, the movement paths of each occupant (taken from their foot movements) was the only factor analyzed.   The degree of accuracy for this type of visual recording was believed to be within a variance of six inch fluctuations (Craik, The Comprehension p.33 App.I).   This variance, relative to the dimensions of the entry hall (12'-8" x 10'-4": 11'-4" ceiling) allowed for a margin of error ranging from 4.8% to 12.5 % (this margin is tested against the pattern's median to arrive at an exact value, found later in this chapter).   Although this variance factor is of a considerable magnitude, the final results of this study are intended to demonstrate the validity of a proxemic analysis of human behavior and architectural form, not the justification of any quantifiable influences attributed to any particular relationship between an occupant and a gestured form.   In the event of a future study intended to reach a conclusion with a more sensitive relationship in proxemics, a more accurate means of observation would be recommended; such as an overhead camera perpendicular to the ground plane or some form of dust-film spread over the floor to record location and frequency of movement patterns.

After the observations of the entry hall were taken and reviewed, there were twenty-seven unique patterns of movement found from the occupants using the space (Canter, Psychology p.152-153 App.I; Barker, Ecological p.28-29 App.J; Rapoport, History p.214-215 App.J).   The patterns were the occupant's movements entering the main entry to the stairs up, to the elevator, to the stairs down, to the President's office, or to the gallery; from the stairs up to the stairs down, to the President's office, out the main entry, or to the gallery; from the elevator to the President's office, out the main entry, or to the gallery; from the stairs down to the President's office, out the main entry, to the stairs up, to the elevator, or to the gallery; from the President's office out the main entry, to the stairs up, to the elevator, to the stairs down, or to the gallery; or from the gallery to the stairs up, to the elevator, to the stairs down, to the President's office, or out the main door.   Of these twenty-seven patterns, six directly relate to the focus of this thesis study: the occupant's proxemic behavior (as influenced by the gestured forms) related to the defined spatial envelope adjacent to the elevator door (Table 2).   Three of those six involved the occupants passing through the main entry: to the stairs up, to the stairs down, and to the President's office (Fig. 9 thru 12).   The fourth pattern involved the occupants circling down the staircase: from the stairs up past the elevator to the stairs

Table 2: Validation of Observations

Pattern Type:	Existing Condition:	Installed Condition:	Adjusted Condition:	Ave.:
Entry through Main Door:	124 paths	186 paths	128 paths	
Percentage of all paths:	24.8 %	28.2 %	22.1 %	
Margin of error:		< 3.4 %	< 2.7 %	**< 3.0 %**
Circulation up & down staircase:	158 paths	170 paths	166 paths	
Percentage of all paths:	31.6 %	29.4 %	29.7 %	
Margin of error:		< 2.2 %	< 1.9 %	**< 2.0 %**
Movement, waiting for elevator:	42 paths	54 paths	42 paths	
Percentage of all paths:	8.4 %	8.5 %	10.8 %	
Margin of error:		< 0.1 %	< 2.4 %	**< 1.3 %**
Stationary Points:	136 points	154 points	86 points	
Points / Path:	**3.24 pt/pa**	**2.85 pt/pa**	**2.05 pt/pa**	
Percent decrease:		12.0 %	36.7 %	

Total Number of Observation Time Samples: 138 (approx. 8-12 minutes each).

Total Number of Individual Movement Paths: 1712 unique movement paths.

Total Number of Individual Patterns of Movement: 27 unique patterns.

down (Fig. 13 thru 16). The fifth pattern involved the reverse of the fourth pattern: from the stairs down past the elevator to the stairs up (Fig. 17). The last and most important pattern involved two behavior types: the movement of the occupants after they entered the main entry as they waited for the arrival of the elevator and the stationary points where the occupants located themselves (in between lateral movements) as they waited for the arrival of the elevator (Fig. 18 thru 24).

Table 2 shows the number of paths (for the six patterns studied) that were recorded during each condition that the entry hall experienced: the initial 'Existing Condition' (before any alterations were done to the space), the 'Installed Condition' (after the four forms were first introduced into the space), and the 'Adjusted Condition' (after two of the four forms were manipulated from their previous 'Installed Condition', refer to Fig. 4). Each pattern type is referenced with a percentage value for these paths in relation to the total number of paths that were recorded, for that pattern, during that condition period. And then the 'margin of error' is calculated, recording the amount of variation each condition period has to the original condition period; this demonstrating that the quantities of pattern types remains consistent throughout this thesis study, validating the accuracy of the time samples collecting a uniform distribution of patterns in each condition period (Ittelson and Proshansky, p.231 App. L). In addition, the sixth pattern type (Entering through the main entry and waiting for the arrival of the elevator) has a category for the number of stationary points recorded during the various condition periods; with a calculated ratio of the number of stationary points per individual path. To state in another way, the ratio is the average number of times that an occupant will pause at a stationary point, while moving about as they wait for the arrival of the elevator (Canter, Psychology p.113-123 App.D). It is interesting to note the last statistic (Percent decrease), which marks the percentage of drop off in the ratio value of one condition period from the previous condition period. This demonstrates that the frequency of the occupant to pause at a stationary point while moving about, significantly drops (from an average of a little more than three times per occupant in the 'Existing Condition' to an average of about two times per occupant in the 'Adjusted Condition') after the adjustments are made to the gestured forms.

The composited median lines in Figure 12 (for the entry patterns through the main door), record the shift of movement patterns over the duration of the study. As an example, the pattern of occupants moving from the main entry to the stairs up, progressively shifts to the left after the forms are installed, and later adjusted. To statistically validate these findings (Hall, Handbook p.102 App.L), the median line drawn for

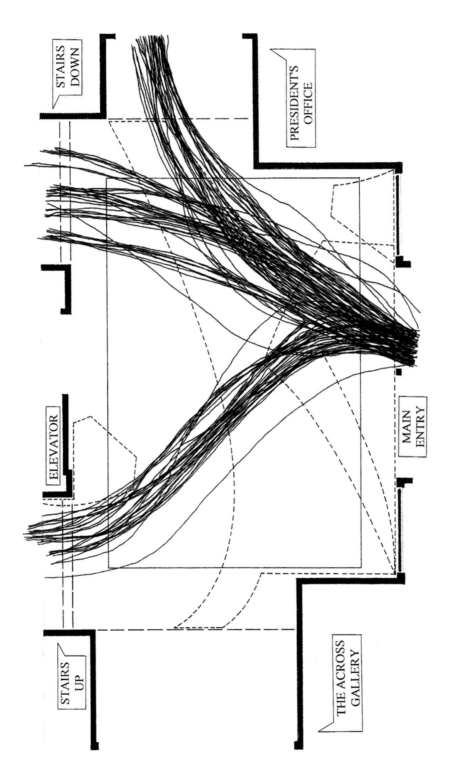

Figure 9:   Entry Patterns through Main Door (Existing Condition)

This is a composite of all of the individual paths (related to three of the twenty-seven different movement patterns) made by the occupants entering the entry hall, during the existing time period before the installation of the four gestured forms.   The three different movement patterns are 'Entry in and up the staircase', 'Entry in and down the staircase', and 'Entry in and into the President's Office'; all used to study the entry hall's spatial conditions.

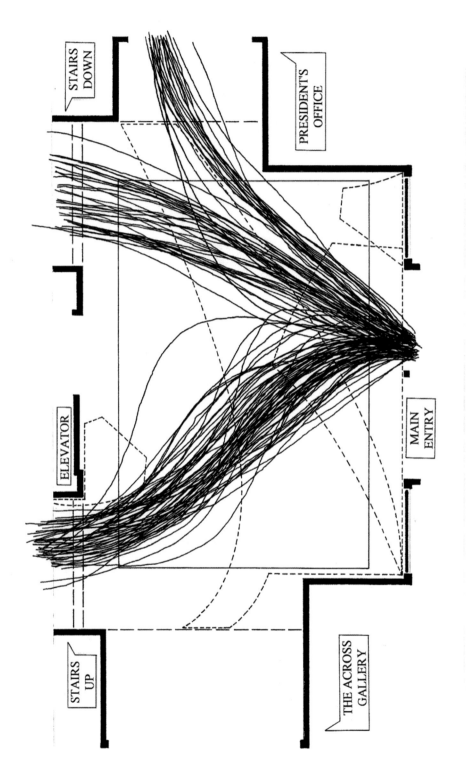

Figure 10: Entry Patterns through Main Door (Installed Condition)

This is a composite of all of the individual paths (related to three of the twenty-seven different movement patterns) made by the occupants entering the entry hall, during the time period following the installation of the four gestured forms. The three different movement patterns are 'Entry in and up the staircase', 'Entry in and down the staircase', and 'Entry in and into the President's Office'; all used to study the entry hall's spatial conditions.

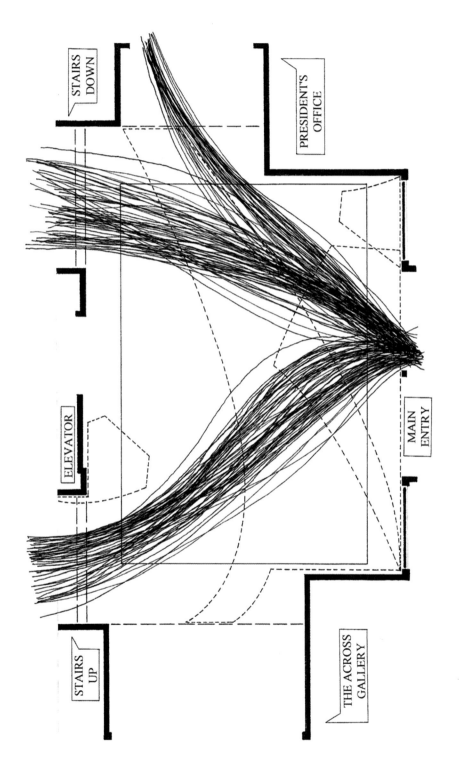

Figure 11: Entry Patterns through Main Door (Adjusted Condition)

This is a composite of all of the individual paths (related to three of the twenty-seven different movement patterns) made by the occupants entering the entry hall, during the time period following the adjustment of two of the four gestured forms. The three different movement patterns are 'Entry in and up the staircase', 'Entry in and down the staircase', and 'Entry in and into the President's Office'; all used to study the entry hall's spatial conditions.

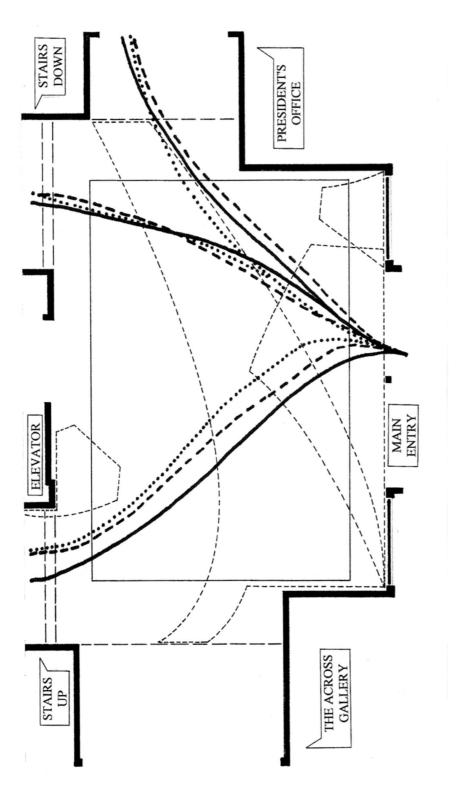

Figure 12: Composited Median Lines for Entry Patterns through Main Door

This is a composite of the three spatial conditions, 'Existing' (dotted lines), 'Installed' (dashed lines), and 'Adjusted' (solid lines). The lines represent a median (excluding ten percent of the paths, to account for atypical variations) of all of the occupant's paths grouped into three movement patterns. Shifts in the movement patterns result from the changing spatial conditions: existing, installed, and adjusted.

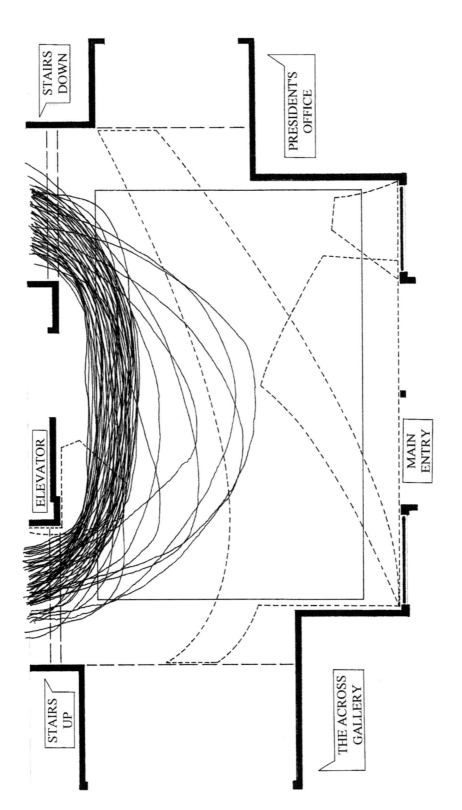

Figure 13: Circulation Pattern Down the Staircase (Existing Condition)

This is a composite of all of the individual paths (related to the movement pattern: Circulation down the Staircase) made by the occupants passing through the entry hall, during the time period before the installation of the four gestured forms. The movement pattern 'Circulation down the Staircase' is used to study the entry hall's spatial conditions of envelopes, perimeters, and relationships.

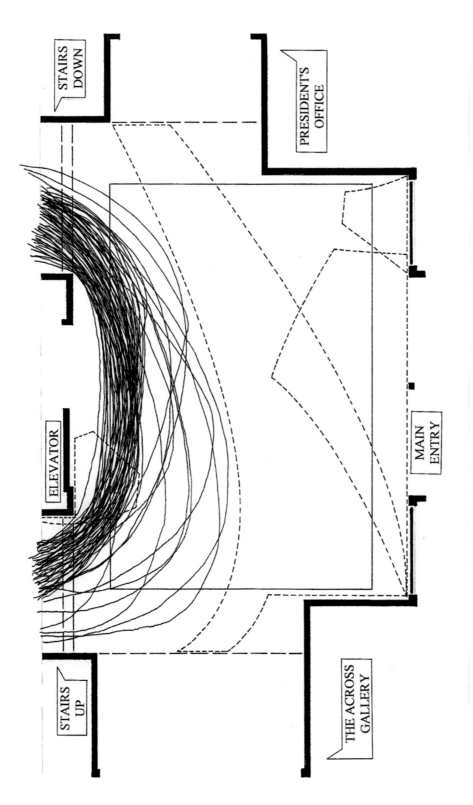

Figure 14: Circulation Pattern Down the Staircase (Installed Condition)

This is a composite of all of the individual paths (related to the movement pattern: Circulation down the Staircase) made by the occupants passing through the entry hall, during the time period following the installation of the four gestured forms. The movement pattern 'Circulation down the Staircase' is used to study the entry hall's spatial conditions of envelopes, perimeters, and relationships.

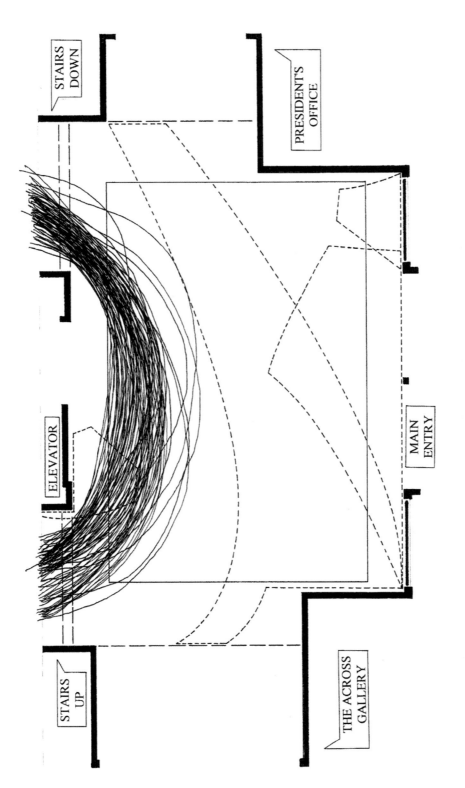

Figure 15: Circulation Pattern Down the Staircase (Adjusted Condition)

This is a composite of all of the individual paths (related to the movement pattern: Circulation down the Staircase) made by the occupants passing through the entry hall, during the time period following the adjustment of two of the four gestured forms. The movement pattern 'Circulation down the Staircase' is used to study the entry hall's spatial conditions of envelopes, perimeters, and relationships.

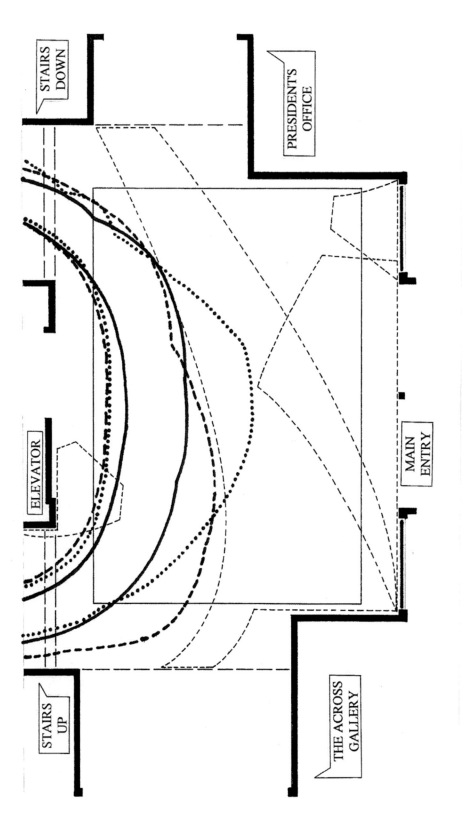

Figure 16: Composited Median Lines for Down the Staircase Pattern

This is a composite of the three spatial conditions, 'Existing' (dotted lines), 'Installed' (dashed lines), and 'Adjusted' (solid lines). The lines represent a median (excluding ten percent of the paths, to account for atypical variations) of all of the occupant's paths grouped into a 'Down the Staircase' movement pattern. Shifts in the movement pattern results from the changing spatial conditions: existing, installed, and adjusted.

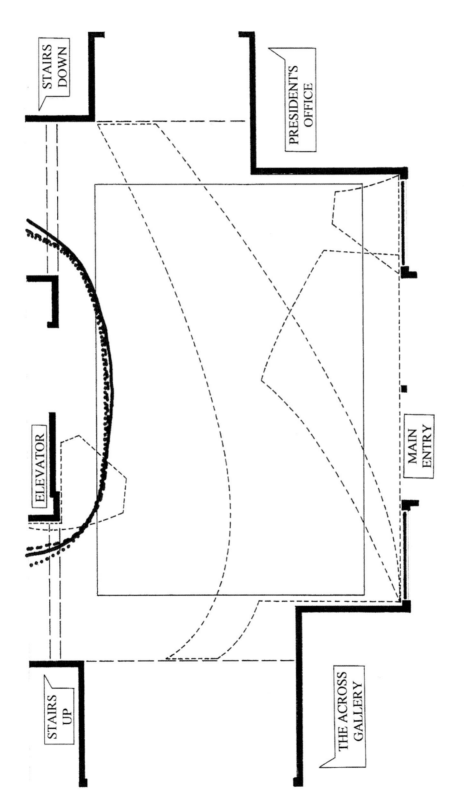

Figure 17: Composited Median Lines for Up the Staircase Pattern

This is a composite of the three spatial conditions, 'Existing' (dotted lines), 'Installed' (dashed lines), and 'Adjusted' (solid lines). The lines represent a median (excluding ten percent of the paths, to account for atypical variations) of all of the occupant's paths grouped into an 'Up the Staircase' movement pattern. Shifts in the movement pattern results from the changing spatial conditions: existing, installed, and adjusted.

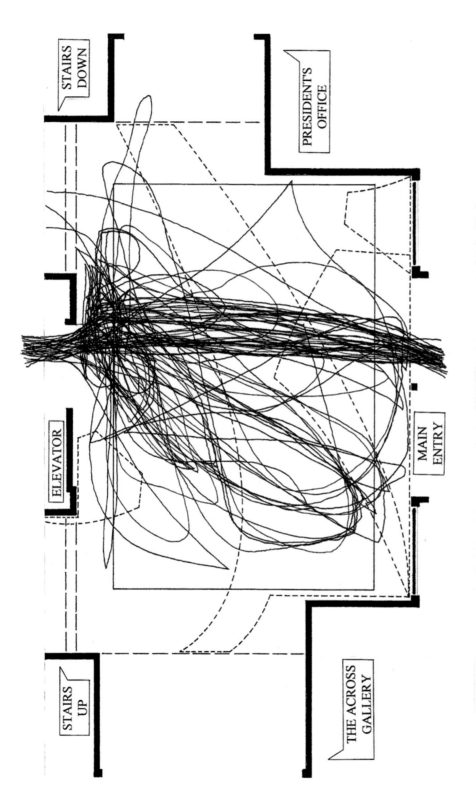

Figure 18: Movement Pattern Waiting for Elevator (Existing Condition)

This is a composite of all of the individual paths (related to the movement pattern: Waiting for Elevator) made by the occupants waiting in the entry hall, during the time period before the installation of the four gestured forms. The movement pattern 'Waiting for Elevator' is used to study the entry hall's spatial conditions of envelopes, perimeters, and relationships.

STAIRS DOWN

PRESIDENT'S OFFICE

ELEVATOR

MAIN ENTRY

STAIRS UP

THE ACROSS GALLERY

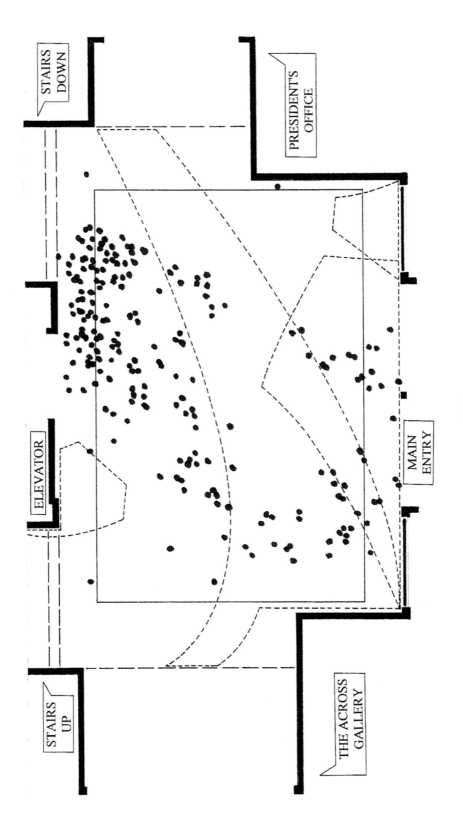

Figure 19: Stationary Points Waiting for Elevator (Existing Condition)

This is a composite of all of the individual points (related to the stationary pattern: Waiting for Elevator) made by the occupants standing in the entry hall, during the time period before the installation of the four gestured forms. The movement pattern 'Waiting for Elevator' is used to study the entry hall's spatial conditions of envelopes, perimeters, and relationships.

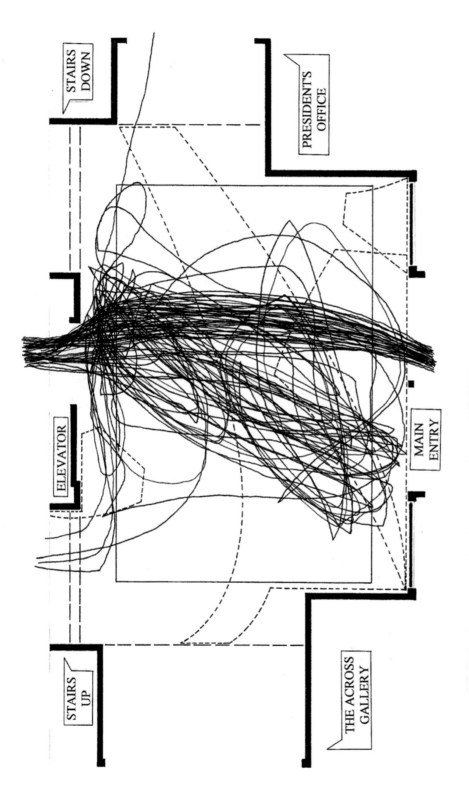

Figure 20: Movement Pattern Waiting for Elevator (Installed Condition)

This is a composite of all of the individual paths (related to the movement pattern: Waiting for Elevator) made by the occupants waiting in the entry hall, during the time period following the installation of the four gestured forms. The movement pattern 'Waiting for Elevator' is used to study the entry hall's spatial conditions of envelopes, perimeters, and relationships.

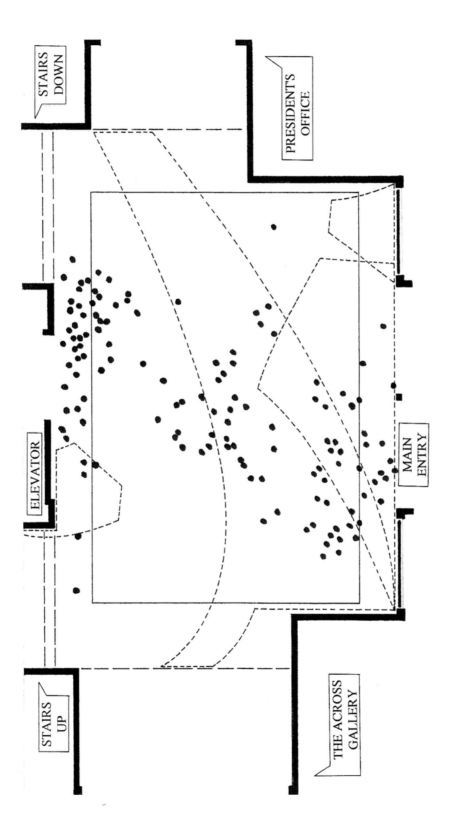

Figure 21: Stationary Points Waiting for Elevator (Installed Condition)

This is a composite of all of the individual points (related to the stationary pattern: Waiting for Elevator) made by the occupants standing in the entry hall, during the time period following the installation of the four gestured forms. The movement pattern 'Waiting for Elevator' is used to study the entry hall's spatial conditions of envelopes, perimeters, and relationships.

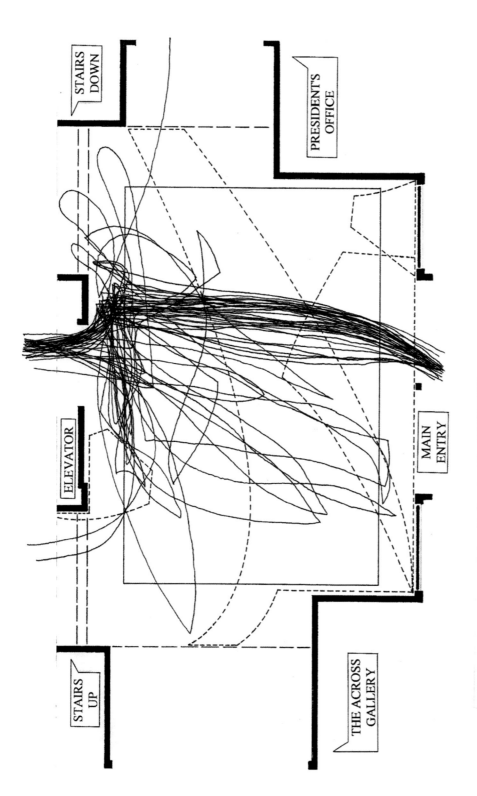

Figure 22:   Movement Pattern Waiting for Elevator   (Adjusted Condition)

This is a composite of all of the individual paths (related to the movement pattern: Waiting for Elevator) made by the occupants waiting in the entry hall, during the time period following the adjustment of two of the four gestured forms.   The movement pattern 'Waiting for Elevator' is used to study the entry hall's spatial conditions of envelopes, perimeters, and relationships.

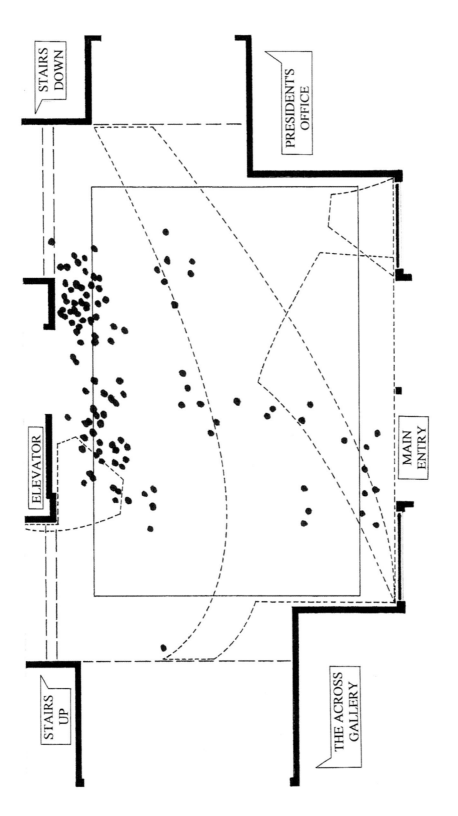

Figure 23: Stationary Points Waiting for Elevator (Adjusted Condition)

This is a composite of all of the individual points (related to the stationary pattern: Waiting for Elevator) made by the occupants standing in the entry hall, during the time period following the adjustment of two of the four gestured forms.   The movement pattern 'Waiting for Elevator' is used to study the entry hall's spatial conditions of envelopes, perimeters, and relationships.

STAIRS
DOWN

PRESIDENT'S
OFFICE

ELEVATOR

MAIN
ENTRY

STAIRS
UP

THE ACROSS
GALLERY

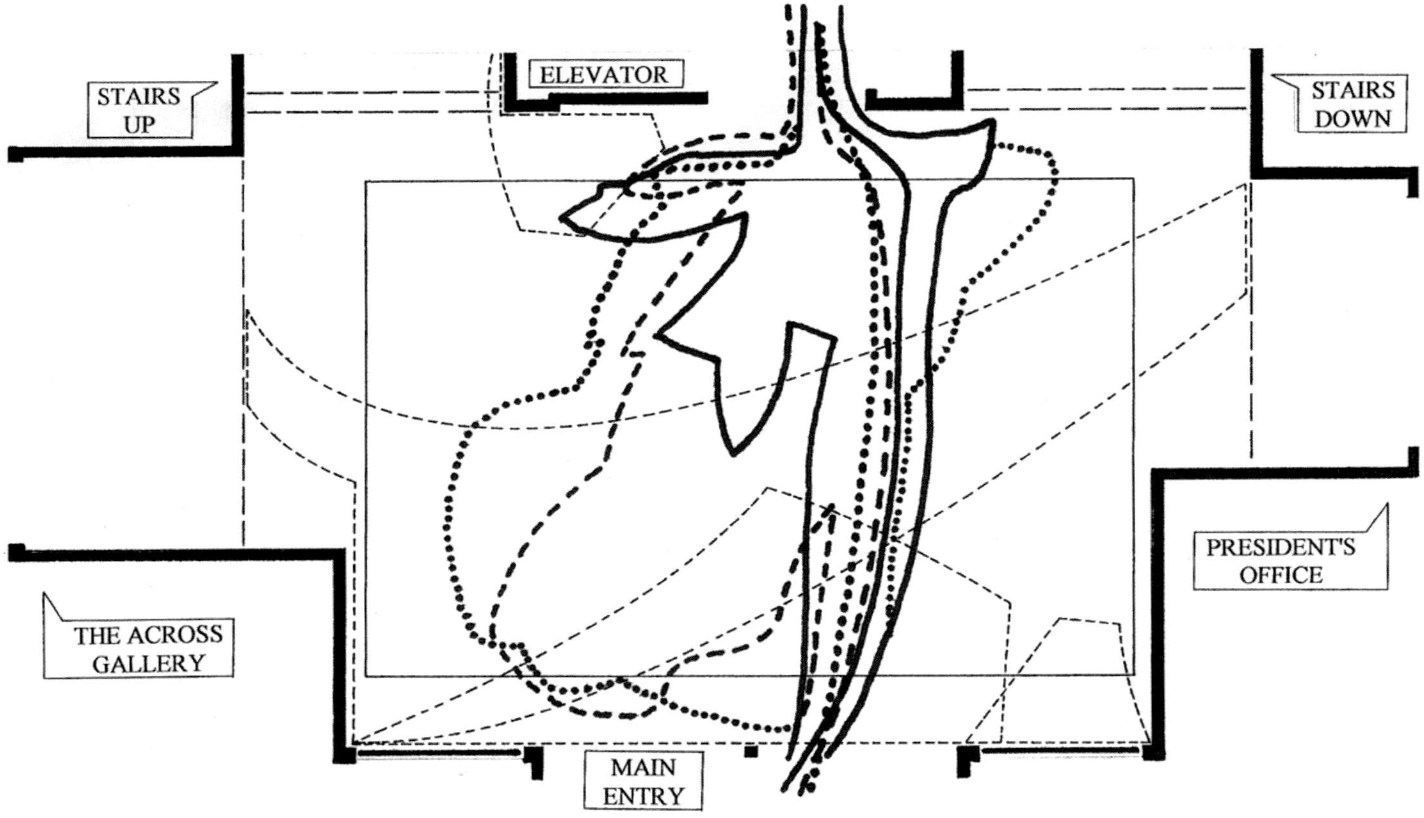
ELEVATOR
STAIRS UP
STAIRS DOWN
PRESIDENT'S OFFICE
THE ACROSS GALLERY
MAIN ENTRY

Figure 24: Composited Median Lines for Pattern: Waiting for Elevator

This is a composite of the three spatial conditions, 'Existing' (dotted lines), 'Installed' (dashed lines), and 'Adjusted' (solid lines). The lines represent a median (excluding ten percent of the paths, to account for atypical variations) of all of the occupant's paths grouped into a 'Waiting for Elevator' movement pattern. Shifts in the movement pattern results from the changing spatial conditions: existing, installed, and adjusted.

each of the three condition periods, was related through a percentage value against the proportionate dimensions (the maps of the entry hall in Fig. 5 thru 24 are drawn at a scale of 3/8" = 1'-0") of the three composite line maps from each condition period (Fig. 9 thru 11). The percentage of shift in the median lines (from the 'Existing' to the 'Adjusted' Conditions, of the patterns to the stairs up) is 60.8 % to the left, in relation to the composite line maps' proportionate dimensions. After the 'margin of error' at a maximum of 12.5 % (as previously stated in this chapter) is deducted from the percentage of shift in the median lines, the result is still a significant difference of 48.3 % shift to the left. In contrast, the movement pattern from the main entry to the stairs down, shifts to the right 16.7 % and then back to the left 5.0 %, over the duration of the study. However, their percentage of shift after the 'margin of error' is factored in, at 4.2 - 11.9 % and 0.0 - 0.2% are both too marginal to insure a significant shift in movement. Therefore, as this example of a statistical analysis demonstrates, the first pattern records a significant shift to the left, of the occupant's movement paths; however the second pattern does not record a significant shift of the movement paths (due to the 'margin of error' present in the observational methods used), even though a shift of the movement paths might have actually existed. Based on this method of statistical validation, only the movement patterns that demonstrate a significant shift in their median lines will be listed and described; for future reference in the next chapter.

Figure 12 records a significant shift of movement paths in the patterns: From the main entry to the stairs up, shifting slightly with the installation of the forms and then a greater shift after the adjustment of two of the four forms. In addition, there is a significant shift inward toward the corner in the pattern from the main entry to the President's office.

Figure 16 records a significant shift of movement paths in the pattern from the stairs up to the stairs down: The median lines shift slightly inward as the occupants pass Form-B during the period of study between the 'Existing' and 'Installed' Conditions; but then shifts much greater outward during the period of study between the 'Installed' and 'Adjusted' Conditions. In addition, the outer perimeter paths (represented by the second set of three lines, below the median lines) of this pattern, show a dramatic shift: first a narrowing of outward swing in movement around the elevator and then, a lateral shift of the deepest point projecting into the center space, first left and then back to the right.

Figure 24 records a significant shift of the movement paths in the pattern from the main entry to waiting for the arrival of the elevator: The median lines (tracing the movement directly in and to the elevator call button) shift to the right over the duration of the study. In addition, the outer perimeter paths (represented by the second set of three lines, circling the median lines) of this pattern, show a dramatic decrease in the 'exploratory' movements of the occupants in the center of the entry hall, while there is an increase in the movement toward Form-B over the duration of the study.

CHAPTER IV: INTERPRETATIONS AND IMPLICATIONS

The observations of the occupants in the entry hall, yielded three general principles about spatial perception and human behavior. The first dealt with 'constricted space' and 'open space' and the perceived functions imposed on them by the occupants. The 'Existing Condition' produced behavior that would collect in the center of the entry hall, obstructing the movement of passing occupants (Fig. 19); this behavior became the focus of this thesis study. The layering of Form-A and Form-C in the front half of the entry hall created a new ceiling plane (at seven feet off the floor plane), constricting the space in relation to the remaining entry hall space. The rear space, primarily defined by the vertical surface of Form-A, but also by the absence of forms, created an open space adjacent to the elevator (Fig. 1). The design intention of these two forms was to create a perceived threshold defining a pocket of space enveloping the elevator core. By doing this, it was anticipated that the occupants would detect this open space and be drawn to it when waiting for the arrival of the elevator. This would pull the waiting occupants away from the center of the entry hall, and allow for the circulating occupants to pass by them without obstruction. However, the observations found a differing behavior resulting from the installation of these two forms. The difference in design expectations and resulting behavior occurred first in the time period following the installation of the four gestured forms. There was a shift in the stationary points for the 'Installed Condition', from the previous 'Existing Condition' (Fig. 19 and 21). The occupants tended to stand closer to the front of the entry hall, under the canopy defined by Form-A and Form-C. These two forms appeared to be drawing the stationary occupants away from the open space and into the constricted space (Wollheim p.38-39 App.F; Rapoport, History p.246-247 App.I); the direct opposite of what the forms were intended to do. After observing this behavior, it was believed to be a result of the occupant's subconscious spatial conditioning that is learned over one's lifetime. The stationary occupants would move toward the constricting perimeter spaces, away from the open space which was viewed by the stationary occupants to be 'more for heavy traffic and the movements of passing occupants' (Wilson p.65-69 App.B; Hall, Handbook p.16-18 App.D). It is only natural for the occupants to have spatial conditioning that realizes the need for more space where there is more movement of people. As recorded in Figure 21, the stationary occupants located quite a bit around the forward projection of Form-C, believed to be drawing the occupants away from the nearby space directly in front of the elevator door, defined by Form-B. An attempt was made to re-direct the behavior patterns of these stationary occupants, to the original design intention; using the observations to guide and inform the adjustments to be made. Adjustments were made to Form-B and Form-C (Fig. 4). The first adjustment, to Form-B, was to have the form lowered to increase the definition of the envelope of space adjacent to the elevator door. By lowering it, a constriction of the space was intended to draw the occupants into this space, similar to what had occurred in the front space with Form-A and Form-C. The second adjustment was intended to aid the first adjustment by lowering the forward projection of Form-C to an 'imposing' height at six and a half feet off the floor. This was believed to repel the stationary occupants away from the larger constricting space under Form-A and Form-C, thereby encouraging the occupants to re-locate in a new position (preferably the newly adjusted space adjacent to the elevator door). It was learned with the independent study of gestured form and activated space (Schlueb, Independent p.2-34 App. M), that there are limits of extreme polarities in the defining of a space's thresholds and envelopes. Therefore, the adjustment of Form-C was intended to push the forward projecting portion of that form beyond the 'comfortable' threshold of constricting space, and into the more severe position, 'imposing' on the occupied space. Figure 23 records a significant shift in the stationary occupant's behavior patterns towards the desired design intention, resulting from the adjustments that were made.

The second of the three general principles observed from the entry hall, was related to the types of paths that were resulting from the occupant's movements. The movement paths were found to be of a specific nature as a result of the tight dimensions in the entry hall (12'-8" width by 10'-4" depth). The paths tended to be smooth curves, connecting the occupant's destination point with their origination point (Fig. 9 thru 11). This seems to be a result that would contradict the implications made by the physical proportions and arrangements within the entry hall. It would be anticipated that a tight space with projecting corners and recessed doorways, would create more linear paths or combinations of linear paths with an angular transition point as occupants 'turned' corners. However, this was not observed to be the case; rather, the paths tended to curve as a result of the short distances between the start and end points, making a smooth transition point as occupants 'rounded' the corners. The hurried movements of the occupants through the entry hall, did not allow for precise changes in directions when confronted with the rapidly unfolding tight context; and therefore resulted in curved transitions of the movement paths.

The last general principle observed, involves the transparent nature of the entry hall's spatial thresholds and perimeter envelope. As referred to earlier in the introductory chapter, the 'Existing Condition' of the entry hall is perceptually transparent at the perimeter surface level. This transparency effects the occupant's foreconscious awareness of the environmental context, however the occupant's subconscious awareness continues to sense the environment's context and responds to it without the occupant's knowledge. The existence of this phenomena became apparent with the observation of the occupant's behavioral responses to the installed forms. The curved paths of movement that the occupants make as they 'round' the corners (referred to in the above paragraph), were recorded to be of a 'safe' proxemic distance from the entry hall's corners in the 'Existing Condition'. However, once the forms were installed in the space, that 'safe' distance narrowed to a 'tighter' distance rounding the corners. Figures 16 and 17 illustrate how Form-B becomes an example of this response, when the occupants pass by the corner on which the form is located. In the 'Installed Condition' the paths are at their 'tightest' distance from the corner, then backing away from the corner in the 'Adjusted Condition'. This response to Form-B is believed to result from the newly installed visual object drawing foreconscious attention to itself. Since the occupant's senses became aware of Form-B, the occupant is able to round the corner 'tighter', with more accuracy and less chance of bumping into the corner as they pass it. In contrast, in the earlier condition without the presence of Form-B, the occupant's foreconscious senses are not stimulated by the transparent nature of the corner's surface perimeter; thereby leaving the occupant's subconscious awareness to judge the proxemic distance of clearance as they pass the corner. Since the occupant's senses are relying on their subconscious awareness, there is a tendency for the occupants to make a 'safe' clearance of the corner; rather than taking the time to assess the distance with their foreconscious awareness (Crick p.205-210 App.B).   In the 'Adjusted Condition' the paths backed away from the corner, resulting from Form-B physically obstructing the previous 'Installed' position's paths.   By adjusting the form to become a physical obstruction on the occupant's movement (as opposed to a conceptual obstruction in the 'Installed Condition'), there was an interesting development between the two types of movement patterns in Figures 16 and 17.   The movement pattern in Figure 16 shows the occupant's paths as they circle down the staircase.   When Form-B was lowered in the 'Adjusted Condition', the median line of movement shifted outside of the original 'Existing Condition'.   This demonstrates that the latest position as a physical obstruction, has 'more' influence of repelling the occupant away from the corner, than when there was no form there at all and the influence was solely from the subconscious awareness of the corner's surface perimeter.   A different development occurred with the movement pattern in Figure 17, which shows the occupant's paths as they climb up the staircase.   In this case, when Form-B was adjusted lower, the median line of movement shifted outward from the 'Installed Condition', but not far enough out to meet with the original 'Existing Condition'.   This demonstrates that the latest position as a physical obstruction, has 'less' influence of repelling the occupant away from the corner, than when there was no form there at all.   By comparing these two patterns, 'circling down' and 'climbing up'; it is evident that these similar patterns yield differing results from the same form in the same position.   The occupant circling down the staircase, perceives more spatial influence from Form-B than the occupant climbing up the staircase.   This may also account for the significant shift in the median lines in Figure 16 and a marginal, almost negligible shift in the median lines in Figure 17.

From these three general principles, based on the observations made of the relationships existing between the enhanced gestured forms and the engaged human occupants in the entry hall space; several interpretations can be made of the connections between behavioral patterns and gestured forms or the occupant's perceptual awareness of proxemics in activated and detached spaces.   The first principle established that proxemic research reveals the degree of influence 'spatial configuration and delineation' can have on human behavior, in addition to the ability to measure the location and extremes of spatial thresholds and envelopes.   While the second and third principles established that this type of research reveals the degree of influence 'form positioning and articulation' can have on human behavior, in addition to the ability to study human subconscious and foreconscious perceptions.   From this research comes a strong argument for the study and adjustment of architectural forms after they have been installed into a space, in order to measure and respond to the occupant's perceptions and behavior patterns. This study could possibly take on a similar critical nature and scientific accuracy as found in such trades as the installation and 'fine tuning' of acoustical tiles in auditoriums; provided that proxemic relationships between body and form are studied with the same degree of intensity and sophistication.

CHAPTER V: CONCLUSION

This thesis was intended to begin a foundation of research and preliminary studies in proxemics and refinement of form and space. In this manner, the work was done attempting only to state an idea or pose a question; not to hypothesize, analyze, or justify any material related to a theory or a premise. Rather, this work is to act as a prototype (or starting point) for a lifetime of observation, sensation, and contemplation. Representing a threshold into a new education, the previous educational years culminated into a driven 'belief' and a desire to test it.

With an emphasis on the subject and intent, this is in no way meant to lessen the validity or sincerity of the research and study in this document. On its own grounds, the observations and interpretations will arrive at end to their inquiry; however, it had to be stated that the prime directive of this document is to develop a tool, from which future referral, renewal, and reassurance may come.

The results of this thesis study did find a significant degree of proxemic influence of form and spatial perception in the movement patterns of the occupants in the Main Building's entry hall (Stea p.13-16 App.G). To return to the initial premise stated in the introductory chapter; it is believed (with the findings of this document) that a proxemic understanding of form, space and body can lead to a perceptual enhancement of the architectonic environment, and ultimately an initial human sense of security through physical and somatic contact in 'total awareness' (Collins p.4 App.F). By studying the 'affects' of gestured forms activating space, on human behavior movement patterns; an understanding of the importance of proxemics in architectural space suggests future studies expanding on this subject. One possible study could include a reversal of the variables, where the human behavior patterns are studied to generate activated spatial thresholds and envelopes, and then the gestured forms are introduced to enhance the existence of those patterns, thresholds, and envelopes (Collins p.6 App.B).

Some of the criticism made at the Thesis Presentation: Final Review, supported the findings and intent of this thesis. While other comments helped to point out theoretical arguments that needed more attention or future exploration. A few excerpts of the criticism are provided to illustrate the direction and concerns of the review panel (Professors Richard Scherr, Theoharis David, John Johansen, James Rossant, and guest juror Chandler Pierce) at the Final Review:

Scherr: Pointed out the validity of a process that 'fine-tunes' the occupant's perceptual awareness of installed forms, after they are installed and behavior patterns are studied.

Johansen: Found the vocabulary (curvilinear based) of the designed forms to be congruent to the organic movements of the occupants (in defiance of the hard-edge corners of traditional orthogonal volumes and spaces).

Scherr: Proposed a future study that could expand on this thesis by exploring 'social use' behaviors of more open public spaces (beyond a simply physical study of the occupant's movement paths).

David: Stated that no great architecture has ever resulted from statistical analysis or research experts studying human interaction with architectural space. He questioned the possibility that this study lost the 'role of the architect': to 'design' a space, founded on intuition, experience, and reaction to functional programming.

Scherr: Pointed out that this study established a set of limits on its intent from the beginning, from which it did not stray throughout the duration of exploration and observation. He commented on the possibility for a larger scope, but confirmed this thesis to be a good start.

" We should make things as simple as possible,

but not simpler. "

Albert Einstein

[Prägnanz Principle]

APPENDICES: RESEARCH PRECEDENT

The following appendices are abstracts taken from research precedents related to this thesis, in the areas of architectural theory, biological and anthropological sciences, aesthetic philosophy, and environmental psychology. These abstracts were selected based on their ability to frame and elaborate on the premise of this study. Most importantly, these abstracts were presented in this manner, to aid the reader in a 'total' conceptual understanding of my thoughts and intentions during the analysis and documentation. Through a more direct and literal description, found in the body of this composition, the reader will arrive at a 'conscious' awareness of my ideology and conclusions. However, having included these abstracts, the reader will be able to access a more indirect and holistic awareness, of the 'subconscious' impressions and influences that structured my mind and perceptions from the onset of this thesis study. Together, using both the conscious and subconscious, the goal of this document is to enable a deeper understanding of my proposed thesis and architectural theories.

APPENDIX A: FORM

[Kipnis, Jeffrey. Post-Analytic Space.]

"In recent decades architectural design has been concerned primarily with developing the architectural object as a historical (PoMo) or sculptural (Decon) form.   Very little attention has been given to exploring the implications of the **architectural object as a generator of space**.   Thus, though striking formal differences distinguish various design attitude today - from Post-Modernism to Deconstructivism - we continue to operate under the assumption that architectural design produces programmed volume, i.e., architectural space understood as organized voids sufficient to meet programmatic demands. Consequently, though the formal and material vocabulary of architecture has been enlarged, the quality of space generated by this expanded vocabulary has remained basically unchanged."

"Beginning with Descartes and culminating with Newton, space has been progressively neutralized as a mathematical concept.   We refer to the class of reduced space, comprising such notions as void, three-dimensional volume, subtractive and additive space, as **analytic space**.

Architectural space, on the other hand, is a much larger and complex class of dynamic relational structures. It includes analytic space, of course, but also extends to object / space relationships with political, social, cultural and even theological implications."

"Unlike the limited case of analytic space, which is neutral and therefore independent of time and place, the possibilities and demands of architectural space, in as much as it is implicated in social and cultural considerations, change with time and place."

"Formal and material articulation do significantly affect architectural space; consequently, the recent efforts to re-articulate analytic space with new forms and materials has improved upon the numbing quality of the most banal analytic space. However, such approaches are not sufficient to explore the possibility of a fundamental reconfiguration of architectural space."

"The concerns of the studio are therefore twofold. First, we will develop non-analytic design processes intended to operate directly with various aspects of architectural space such as sectional space, relational space, threshold space and contextual / urban space. Then, recalling that architectural space must respond to cultural changes to maintain its relevance, we will consider the possibility that today's political, economic, technological and social environment demands a new urban architectural space."

"In the second of our concerns, therefore, we will consider the implications for program of a shift from the analytic space of the **structured event** to a **post-analytic** space able to meet programming requirements but in addition capable of engendering a relevant **Event-Structure**. Event-Structure is a concept which names the exorbitance, the spatial excess necessary to stage and condition the unforeseen flux of small scale social, economic and political encounters characteristic of a relevant contemporary architectural space. Event-structures operate over and above the choreographed coordination of program, form and void typical of the analytic architecture of the structured event."

[Kipnis, Jeffrey. Of Objectology. p.102]
"My work has led me to speculate about something which might be termed the 'mind' or, better, the 'will' of the object. It shows up in the following relationship, which I call the axiom of Objectology:

$$< u(o) > = < u(s) >$$

Though it would not be entirely correct, it can reasonably be interpreted as saying: the quantity of the **will of the object** is in dynamic equilibrium with the quantity of the **will of the subject**."

"It says that if, in the investigation of the repeal of transcendentality, we are going to continue to operate with any conceptual structure employing notions like mind or will, then it is no longer tenable to confine those concepts to animate things, particularly man. We must begin logically to think the reality of the will of the object."

"The will of the subject is obedient to the **will of the object**; that is, the equilibrium is dominated by the dynamics of the will of the object rather than that of the subject."

"This means that the architectural object produces the architectural subject as obedient to it; architecture produces the architect rather than vice versa."

[Kipnis, Jeffrey. Of Objectology. p.104]

"To continue, Derrida, in Of Grammatolgy, was able to disrupt the operation of the 'metaphysic of presence' in written texts in part by focusing on the physicality, the **objectivity**, of writing - correct spelling, spacing, punctuation, capital letters, etc. In other words, he uses the fact that language, whether written or spoken, depends on the disappearance, the becoming invisible of its objectivity to express the presence of its meaning. In a sense, that is the very definition of **meaning**.

Derrida then takes advantage of the fact that the disappearance is never complete. We might say that the metaphysic of encounter with language is such as to repress the **textuality**. Deconstruction derives from and thrives on the fact that the repression can de facto never be total; therefore, there will always be a return of the repressed, an insinuation of the consequences of residual physicality into language which will always disrupt language's goal of achieving univocal meaning."

[Kipnis, Jeffrey. Of Objectology. p.105]

"The 'self-evidency' of architecture as a visual art troubles me, for it sets a specific agenda which does not seem to me empirically justifiable, and which therefore is another manifestation of moralization. We live with an **architectural object** for a very long time, in frequent repetition, etc. Therefore its content does not have to unfold itself in a moment, in a day, in a visit or a photograph. In short, it does not have to be beautiful, even in the very permissive sense of the term as we use it today. Its orders of complexity can be much more elaborate, possibly even to the point of requiring more than a lifetime to unfold."

[Kipnis, Jeffrey. Towards a New Architecture. p.43-44]

"For, **DeFormation**, on the other hand, architecture's most important contribution to the production of new forms and to the inflection of political space continues to be aesthetic. Far from being Blank, DeFormation perceives the modernist language of **InFormation** as nothing less than historical reference and the use of projected images no more than applied ornament. Instead, DeFormation searches for Blankness by extending Modernism's exploration of monolithic form, while rejecting essentialist appeal to

Platonic / Euclidean / Cartesian geometries.   Pointing is accomplished in the aesthetics; the forms transform their context by entering into undisciplined and incongruous formal relationships."

"As is always the case in architectural design theory, **DeFormation** is an artifact, a construction of principles that have emerged after the fact from projects by diverse architects that were originally forged with different intentions and under different terms and conditions."

[Kipnis, Jeffrey. Towards a New Architecture. p.46-48]

"(1) An emphasis on **abstract, monolithic architectural form** that broaches **minimal direct references** or resemblance and that is **alien to the dominant architectural modes** of a given site;   (2) the development of **smoothing affiliations with minor organisations** operating within a context that are **engendered by the intrinsic geometric, topological and / or spatial qualities of the form**."

"the evolution of one last principle must be traced."

"**to avoid** both the **continuous, homogenous space** of the free plan and the **finite, hierarchical space** of more traditional sectional strategies."

"In effect rendering the primary space of the building **interstitial**."

"was embedded as in incongruent object into the urban object massing."

"achieved an extreme detachment of sectional space from the massing."

"to continue to develop methods for generating **affiliative, monolithic forms** and, as well, to develop these sectional ideas.   Our **Event-Structure** called for a large **DeFormed envelope** within which three independently DeFormed theatres floated as **sectional objects**."

"to render all of the spaces in the building **interstitial** and / or **residual** and **to activate them** into a non-hierarchical differential structure."

"The two major **sectional themes** of DeFormation began to emerge.   First, as far as possible, the **section space of the building should not be congruent with the internal space implied by the monolith**. Secondly, wherever possible, res**idual, interstitial and other artifactual spaces should be emphasised over primary spaces**.   Because the **box-within-box section** is effective at producing both of these effects, it is often the tactic of choice though by no means the only one possible."

"debates revolve around **design techniques** for producing **smoothing affiliations**.   Because such affiliations require that loose links be made among dominant and contingent organisations operating within a context,"

"rely entirely on the **intrinsic** contextual affiliations engendered"

"in each case, most of the links were **unplanned** and occurred only after grafting the project to the site."

"**Anexact geometry** is the study of non-analytic forms (i.e., forms that are not describable by an algebraic expression) yet that show a high degree of internal self-consistency. **Non-developable** surfaces cannot be flattened into a plane."

"Neither **pure figure** nor **pure organization folds** link the two; they are monolithic and often non-representational, replete with interstitial and residual spaces, and intrinsic to non-developable surfaces."

"**folding** holds out the possibility of generating field organizations that negotiate between the infinite homogeneity of the grid and the hierarchical heterogeneity of finite geometric patterns,"

"when exercised as a process on two or more organizations simultaneously, **folding** is a potential **smoothing strategy**."

"none of the architects who make use of Thom's fold diagrams, for example, make any claim, as far as I know, to inscribing the four-dimensional **event space** that the diagrams depict for mathematicians in the resultant architecture;"

"The resulting **drawings** create the representational illusion that these two **organizations** have been **folded**."

"The **figure of the fold**, a quotation of sections cut through a Thomian diagram, appears on the tops of the building to effect the **weak**, cross-disciplinary links of which Eisenman is so fond."

"folds it in a process reminiscent of **origami** in order to **deform** the type and to produce multiple **residual spaces**."

"In order to avoid the pitfalls of **expressionist processes**, such **diagrams** offer a level of discipline to the work. Using these diagrams as a source of regulating **lines**, so to speak, allows the architect to design with greater rigor."

"such diagrams are neither purely figural nor purely abstract. They therefore hold the potential to generate **weak, resemblance effects**. Finally, the multiple and disjoint formal organizations that compose these compound diagrams themselves have many of the desired **spatial characteristics** described previously on sections."

[Kuspit, Donald B. Clement Greenberg: Art Critic. p.96-97]

"Like Berenson and Kant, Greenberg favors disinterested, abstract, pure art - an art, in fact, which truly realizes the nature of art, expresses its essence free of the accidents of personal and cultural existence. In other word, an art for art' sake. Abstract art does what art is truly supposed to do, viz., **transcend life, refine its charge and clarify its purpose**-articulate in pure way its general sense of purpose, free of any particular purpose. As such, abstract art is classic art, for it impersonally fulfills the general purpose of art, while Surrealism and Expressionism are romantic art, in that they give freer rein to personal and cultural factors. Where a classic art deals with these indirectly, through the veil of transcendence, a romantic art means to deal with these as directly as possible, without thereby destroying the art in art, although at times it seems willing to do so."

"For Greenberg, the key distinction is between art's universal aesthetic potential and its personal and cultural reality. The latter must be cleared away that the former **may be felt**. It was abstract art which renewed this universal aesthetic potential in our day, whatever the personal and cultural conditions of its origination. Whatever charm, signs of worldly involvement, descriptive innuendos-life references-it has are incidental to, or at best the launching pad for, its aesthetic power."

[Kuspit, Donald B. Clement Greenberg: Art Critic. p.108-109]

"Thus a kind of paradigm of creativity emerges in Greenberg, plotting the relationship of **form** and **feeling**. The task of art is **to create sensibility**, i.e., to associate particular feeling with particular form so that the latter unmistakably, persuasively conveys the former. But once created, the style which articulates the sensibility becomes **a look** which can be manipulated independently of it. The style can be used to create effects alien to the emotion it embodies. It becomes purely instrumental, and its original overtone of feeling-or **'resonance,'** as Greenberg calls it at one point-diminishes, and is finally altogether drained off by the generalization of the style, making it easy to apply. Forceful feeling becomes slick sentiment, or is entirely forgotten, and the style, as well as the sensibility it articulates, becomes bankrupt. To continue to have 'effect,' it becomes a stunt, then a gimmick. For Greenberg, only the direct expression of emotional depth can renew sensibility, work against the grotesqueries of decadence. Only raw emotion can make art **'difficult'** and **'transcendental'** again, beyond the reach of the slickness that creates the illusion of universal accessibility, the magic trick of good design."

"Form without feeling leads to arbitrariness as much as feeling without form For Greenberg, if art is not dialectical, it is arbitrary, and ultimately chaotic."

[Kuspit, Donald B. Clement Greenberg: Art Critic. p.127]

"the psychoanalytical explanation, which sees the creation of 'effective' style as a subtle process of emotional repression. Emotion **'escapes'** through **'form'** which seems alien to it: it is identified with abstract or **'reduced' form**, even in illusionistic art. The emotion associated with the illusion is not the same as aesthetically released emotion. Without the transference of emotion from the illusion to the forms that constitute it, there is no aesthetic exhilaration. In a sense it is the artist's task to make these abstract forms concrete to consciousness while making the illusion seem abstract to it. Without this dialectical conversion there is no **emotional transference**."

[Kuspit, Donald B. Clement Greenberg: Art Critic. p.133]

"The truth is not what is felt but what works and is consistent with itself. The result is a split in consciousness, between the conative and the cognitive, the **subjective** and the **objective**. In the end we fall prey to a kind of collective schizophrenia. Greenberg, while seeming to accept the idea that art might end the split between the subjective and objective, in fact reinforces the split by emphasizing the **objective** in art at the expense of the **subjective** that might be in it. The surest guarantee that art exists is the thought of the medium, making its presence 'categorical' for the subject who makes art his **object**. Art must become completely knowable and objective by concerning itself only with 'what works and is consistent with itself.' The medium alone is consistent with itself; as such it is the objective ground of art. The critic is a connoisseur of the medium, pointing out its consistent use as proof of artistic presence. Not inconsistent feeling, which does not consistently work to guarantee the existence of anything, but consistent thought about the medium works to make art. Feeling always goes wrong, because it looks for its own validation, not the validation of the **object** it is directed to or the **subject** arises in-further indication that modern art ought to be about the **medium**, not about validating **feeling**."

[Kuspit, Donald B. Clement Greenberg: Art Critic. p.148]

"Suffice it to say that the ultimate critical experience of self-certain taste is quasi divine. It is not simply a **transcendental experience**, but proof of the critic's **transcendent being**, to use another Kantian distinction. Such apotheosis-the critic as the god he would like to think he is-seems to make the artist his ministering angel, and art a kind of music of the spheres only the critic can hear, a mysterious learning in which didactically instructs his 'consensus.' For Greenberg criticism is **'an act of intuition'** that 'stops with itself...an end in itself, contains its value in itself and rests in itself.' In other words, it is the self-reflexive activity of a god, his narcissistic self-justification. Taste is the mirror the critic holds up to his perfect being, as well as the sign of his 'jurisdiction."

" 'Things that purport to be art do not function, do not exist, as art until they are experienced through taste. Until then they exist only as empirical phenomena, as **aesthetically arbitrary objects** or **facts**.' Unless it lives in the atmosphere of taste, art has no being as such. This dialectical epistemology, incidentally, is not without validity in its assumption that the object is not really the **'object'** unless it is known by the **subject**."

[Kuspit, Donald B. Clement Greenberg: Art Critic. p.152]

"**Modernism**, which rationalizes itself as a scientifically empirical aesthetics, is in fact as ultimately absurd and irrational a conception of art, including abstract art, as it implies art is of life."

[Freud, Sigmund. Civilizations and Its Discontents. p.71-72]

"Freud first used the word **'sublimation'** in an 1897 letter to Fliess. He described the fantasies of the hysteric as 'protective structures, sublimations of the facts, embellishments of them, and at the same time serve for self-exoneration.' More relevant to the purposes of this paper, the next use occurs in the 1905 Three Essays on the Theory of Sexuality. He explicitly associates sublimation with art, as though art was his major example. He seems to suggest that sublimation is originally artistic, or more accurately, aesthetic. Sexual curiosity, he writes, can be 'diverted (**'sublimated'**) in the direction of art if its interest can be shifted away from the genitals on to the shape of the body as a whole.' This is a shift from content to form-from a body part with overt sexual purpose to the body's form, which becomes covertly sexual in the process. That is, it is a shift from a specifically sexual interest in the genitals to a generally erotic interest in the body. The eroticizing of the body's form, so that the body seems desirable as a whole, is in effect the **first sublimation**-one might say aetheticization-of sexuality. If we put this together with the 1897 sentence, it seems possible to argue that Freud is asserting, however unwittingly, that the displacement of sexual interest to art is hysterical in character. This suggests that the interest in artistic form in and for itself, that is, in denial of its sexual connotations, is hysterical. However, later in the Three Essays Freud speaks more broadly and definitively: 'sublimation enables excessively strong excitation arising from particular sources of sexuality to find an outlet and use in other fields, so that a not inconsiderable increase in psychical efficiency results from a disposition which in itself is perilous...The multifariously perverse sexual disposition of childhood can accordingly be regarded as the source of a number of our virtues.' In his 1915 essay on narcissism, Freud offers his most comprehensive definition of sublimation. It 'is a process that concerns object-libido and consists in the instinct's directing itself towards an aim other than, and remote from, that of sexual satisfaction; in this process the accent falls upon deflection from sexuality...**sublimation** is a way out, a way by which those (instinctual) demands can be met without involving repression.' If we trace the path of the concept of sublimation from 1897-1915, we see that it has changed from a defense to a mode of adaption As Anna Freud states, **'sublimation**, i.e., the displacement of the instinctual aim in conformity with higher social values, presupposes the acceptance or at least the knowledge of such values, that is to say, presupposes the existence of the superego' and as such 'could not be employed until relatively late in the process of development.' It 'pertains rather to the study of the normal than that of neurosis.' The transitional process is equally normal. An object becomes transitional when it serves the purpose of helping the infant make the difficult transition from **unconscious fusion** with the mother to **consciousness of its separateness** from the mother - **its difference from** the mother as well as **other objects.** Winnicott calls this a transition from the me to the not-me. Both are implicated in the transitional object, so that the question as to whether it is artistically invented or cognitively discovered by the infant is meaningless to it. It has in effect done both, with no sense of the difference between them. As Winnicott says, the infant regards the object 'without reference to the object's state of being either subjective or objectively perceived.' It sees no contradiction between these states."

[Wollheim, Richard. The Image in Form: Selected Writings of Adrian Stokes. p.116-117]
"The basic architecture of the visual arts depends upon the many alternations such as repose and movement, density and space, light and dark, that underlie composition, none of which can be divorced initially from the sense of **interacting textures**. Aesthetic appreciation has an identical root: it is best nurtured by architecture, the inescapable Mother of the Arts. Indeed, the ideal way to experience painting in Italy is first to examine olive terraces and their farms, then fine streets of the plain houses, before entering a gallery."

"Now, if we are to allot pre-eminence in **aesthetic form** to an underlying **image of the body**, we must distinguish two aspects of that image, or, rather, two images which are joined in a work of art. There is the aspect which leads us to experience from art a feeling of **oneness with the world**, perhaps not dissimilar from the experience of mystics, of infants at the breast and of everyone at the deeper points of sleep. We experience it to some extent also from **passion, manic states, intoxication**, and perhaps during a rare moment in which we have truly accepted death; above all, from states of **physical exaltation and catharsis** whose rhythm has once again transcribed the world for our possession and for its possessiveness of us; but only in contemplating works of art, as well as nature, well all our faculties have full play, will we discover this kind of contemplation in company with the counterpart that eases the manic trend."

"**Space** is a homogeneous medium into which we are drawn and freely plunged by many representations of visual art; at the same time it is the mode of order and distinctiveness for separated **objects**."

[Wollheim, Richard. The Image in Form: Selected Writings of Adrian Stokes. p.122-123]
"It is therefore important to discover in art the recounting of all aspects that the body has possessed, the **inside** (as seen from without) as well as the **outside**. (Thus glimmering or tufted finery that clothes many somber Rembrandt figures can mirror the character of inner objects for whose state the individual is massively responsible. It is for such communication, however recondite, that we scan good portraits. At any rate we learn to see the **spirit**, the animation, in terms of art's inoffensive material. That material **stands** for the body whether or not it has been used to **represent** the body. Art, truly seen, is never ghostly; and art, truly seen, does not so much educate us about animation, about the mind or spirit, about the intentions of others good or bad in which we find a source of persecutory feeling or of trust, as about the resulting body-person, **about the embodiment** that is much more than an embodiment because bodily

attributes have always been identified with those intentions. A painting of the **nude**, therefore, is but one of the corporeal lessons set by art. There sense in which **all art is of the body**, particularly so in the eyes of those who accept that the painted surface and other media of art represent as general form, which their employment particularizes, the actualities of the hidden psychic structure made up of evaluations and fantasies with **corporeal content**."

"Often in a talk about art we get at least a partial division of formal attributes from representation. We say the formal relationships organize the representation, the images, on view. That's the **traditional approach**. On the other hand, in the theory of **Significant Form**, form is isolated from imagery, from the construction of likeness in visual terms. I am going to argue that **formal relationships** themselves entail a representation or imagery of their own though these likenesses are not as explicit as the images we obtain from what we call the **subject-matter**. When later I shall refer to Cezanne's Bathers in the National Gallery, I shall suggest that there is far more imagery in this picture than the imagery of nudes in a landscape."

"It suggested an image for an amalgam of experiences, even though that impression had not been achieved by the creation of a correspondence with recognized events as is the case where you have a subject-matter."

APPENDIX B: PERCEPTION

[Gibson, J. J. The Senses Considered as Perceptual Systems. p.59-61]

"A living animal can orient itself in many ways. All of these are **orientations to the environment**, but to different features of the environment, such as gravity, or the sun in the sky, or a sudden noise, or a mate."

"In this chapter, we will consider the simplest kind of orientation, to the direction up-down and to the plane of the ground. Along with this goes a basic type of perception on which other perceptions depend, that is, the detection of the **stable permanent framework of the environment**. This is sometimes called the perception of 'space,' but that term implies something abstract and intellectual, whereas what is meant is something concrete and primitive - a dim, underlying, and ceaseless awareness of what is permanent in the world."

"The primary kind of orientation is to **gravity**. In the water or on the land all animals respond to the pull of the earth, and most of the multicellular animals have developed a special organ for detecting the direction of gravity when resting. In its simplest for it is called statocyst."

"the hairs being stimulated by a weight which can be displaced relative to the sac."

"The **statolith** is literally a stone, being composed of calcium carbonate, and is quite heavy relative to the fluid and tissue around it."

[Gibson, J. J. The Senses Considered as Perceptual Systems. p.97-98]

"The sensibility of the individual to the world adjacent to his body by the use of his body will here be called the **haptic system**. The word haptic comes from a Greek term meaning 'able to lay hold of.' It operates when a man or animal **feels things with his body or its extremities**. It is not just the sense of skin pressure. It is not even the senses of pressure plus the sense of kinesthesis."

"since the inputs available for **perception** may not be the same as the inputs available for **sensation**. There are inputs for perception, and also for the control of performance, that have no discoverable sensations to correspond. The haptic system, then, is an apparatus by which the individual gets information about both the environment and his body. He feels an object relative to the body and the body relative to an object. It is the perceptual system by which animals and men are literally in touch with the environment. When we say figuratively that a man is in touch with the environment by looking or listening, the metaphor is something to think about, but we can put this off until later."

"Aristotle's sense of touch, the fifth sense, did not seem to be unitary on careful examination. For one thing, it had no organ like the eye, ear, nose, or mouth, and the skin did not fit the idea of a sense organ. So it got subdivided. The first extra sense to be split off from touch was the muscle sense. It was then argued that temperature was a different quality from touch, and that pain also was different. Then warm was separated from cold when it was discovered that the skin of man contained different groups of spots yielding characteristic sensations of warmness and coldness. Spots for pressure and for prickly pain could also be mapped out, and they did not coincide. The sensitivity of the joints was then discovered, and this, with or without the muscle sense, was called **kinesthesis**. But what about feelings of strain, or of deep pressure? What about cutaneous motion? Some argued that the feelings of the body were so much allied as to be subsumed under one name- Boring has called it **somaesthesis**."

[Gibson, J. J. The Senses Considered as Perceptual Systems. p.100-102]

"The capacity of vibrissae, hairs, claws, and horns **to feel things at a distance** is not different in principle from the ability of a man to use a cane or probe to detect the mechanical encounters at the end of the artificial appendage to his hand. The use of **tools**, from sticks, clubs, and rakes to more elaborate ones like screwdrivers and pliers or even fishing rods and tennis rackets, is probably based on a perceptual capacity of the body that is found in other animals. The remarkable fact is that when a man touches something with a stick he feels it at the end of the stick, not in the hand. This is a difficulty for the theory of sensation-based perception; it requires some such postulate as **the projecting of sensations outward from the body**. But we entertain the hypothesis that information for the mechanical disturbance at the end of the stick is obtained by the hand as a perceptual organ, including information about the length and direction of the stick. The sensations in the hand itself are irrelevant. The surface of an organism, it should be remembered, is actually a **boundary** between the organism and its environment, and the boundary is **not always or everywhere as clean-cut** as the hairless human philosopher tends to think."

"It has been observed in previous chapters that the upright body posture depends on a hierarchy of postures- of the head relative to the trunk, of the trunk relative to the legs, and thus of the whole system relative to the ground. It was noted that this system cofunctions with the vestibular orientation of the head relative to gravity, so that contact with the ground and orientation to gravity make a superordinate system. It should now be evident that the posture of each and every body member is an elaboration of this system (see Figure 6.2). For the **angular position** of every bone of the body out to the extremities is literally articulated with the body frame, and thus anchored to the direction of gravity and to the plane of the substratum. The sensitivity of the joints to their angles is evidently of crucial importance for this elaboration. In this way an extremity can be oriented to both the **frame of the body** and the **framework of space**, even in the absence of vision. The disposition of all the bones, at any moment in time, can be thought of as a sort of branching vector space in the larger space of the environment, specified by the set of the angles at all joints **relative** to the main axes of the body."

[Gibson, J. J. The Senses Considered as Perceptual Systems. p.109]
"The evidence strongly suggests that **muscle sensitivity** is irrelevant for the perception of space and movement, whereas **joint sensitivity** is very important for it. In short, we detect the angles of our joints, not the lengths of our muscles. It is not often realized, even by anatomists, that it is the function of a joint not merely to permit mobility of the articulated bones but also to register the relative position and movement of the bones. In the old terminology, each joint is a 'sense organ.' Here it is called a receptive unit in a hierarchy of units."

[Gibson, J. J. The Senses Considered as Perceptual Systems. p.122]
"The question of which sense to believe in, whether to trust what one **feels** or what one **sees** when the data conflict has never been answered, although it is still being debated (e.g., Harris, 1963). Perhaps both processes can occur - both spontaneous normalizing and cross-sensory reduction of discrepancy."

[Gibson, J. J. The Senses Considered as Perceptual Systems. p.160]

"There is evidence to suggest that a visual system can have good acuity for distinguishing among the forms of **motion** in ambient light without necessarily having high acuity for distinguishing among **static** forms."

"but we are so preoccupied with **form** as such that we take for granted the subtleties of transformation in our field of view. In varying degrees, then, vision makes possible the perception of **objective** motion. But it also is used for the detection and control of **subjective** movement, that is, the movement of the animal himself in the environment."

[Gibson, J. J. The Senses Considered as Perceptual Systems. p.175-177]

"The compulsory convergence of the centers of both eyes on the same bit of the world is a characteristic of the primates and man, and it probably goes with the effort to use a separate and distinct kind of information about the layout of things, that given by the disparity of the overlapping arrays which coexists along with their identity."

"The human retina has a **fovea** that corresponds to the **subjective** center of clear vision, or the external point of fixation. That beam of light which falls on the fovea determines the gaze-line or what is sometimes vaguely called the line of sight. Certain direction-from-here, in which things need to be seen, are more important than other directions, depending on the animal's way of life. The general direction **ahead** is often more significant than the direction **behind**, as already noted. The direction **above** may be more significant for some species than the direction **below**, but this significance can be reversed for other species. The directions to the right and to the left would seem to be equally significant for all species. Evenly dispersed panoramic vision in all directions is therefore wasteful, and some animals adapted to this fact by concentrating the resources of each eye, that is, by a tendency toward foveation. But note that the full development of frontal eyes with foveas must be accompanied by the development of the ability to **look** - that is, to explore the optic array by scanning it. If panoramic vision is restricted, the ability to look around must be substituted. The parts of the array must be fixated in succession; there must be exploration and selection of certain **items of interest** to the **neglect of other items**. This is nothing less than **visual attention**; it demands what physiologists have called 'voluntary' eye movements, although the term is unfortunate. The exploratory fixations can be carried out by the eyes alone in vertebrates with freely mobile eyes; otherwise they must be performed with the head, as happens in many birds, or with the whole body, as happens in many arthropods."

[Gibson, J. J. The Senses Considered as Perceptual Systems. p.177]

"The nervous equipment necessary for the delicate balancing of the eye muscles in this automatic converging and conjugating must obviously be exact and subtle. If convergence is to be maintained at all times, the system has to register even the slightest mismatch of detail at the two foveas so as to correct it. The center of the pattern of the optic array entering one eye has to coincide with the center of the pattern of the array entering the other eye. The forms at the two foveas have to be congruent forms, and **the system has to detect incongruence of form** in order to maintain convergence. As the eyes move upward from the hands, to the ground nearby, to the distant horizon, the convergence of the gaze-lines must always be relaxed just enough to eliminate disparity of pattern at the foveas."

[Gibson, J. J. The Senses Considered as Perceptual Systems. p.267-268]
"the available stimulation surrounding an organism has structure, both **simultaneous** and **successive**, and that this structure depends on sources in the outer environment. If the invariants of this structure can be registered by a perceptual system, the constants of neural input will correspond to the constants of stimulus energy, although the one will not copy the other. But then **meaningful information** can be said to exist inside the nervous system as well as outside. The brain is relieved of the necessity of constructing such information by any process- innate rational powers (**theoretical nativism**), the storehouse of memory (**empiricism**), or form-fields (**Gestalt theory**). The brain can be treated as the highest of several centers of the nervous system governing the perceptual systems."

"The education of the perceptual systems depends mainly on the **individual's history of exposure to the environment**. So there are really three questions: How much does perceiving depend on organs? How much does it depend on growth? How much does it depend on experience?"

[Gibson, J. J. The Senses Considered as Perceptual Systems. p.276-278]
"The idea that **'space'** is perceived whereas **'time'** is remembered lurks at the back of our thinking."
"It has often been pointed out that **memory** has quite different manifestations. To **recognize** is not the same as to **recall**."
"Nevertheless, both are considered forms of memory and the theory of traces requires that, even for **recognition**, the present input must somehow **retrieve the stored image** of the earlier experience. If the input matches, recognition occurs; if not, recognition fails."
"The **'successions'** of stimulation include both **non-changes** and **changes**, and therefore the detection of same is no less primary than the detection of different. One is the reciprocal of the other and neither requires an act of mental comparison. This is quite evident in the simplest possible case of recognition, in which one encounter with an object is followed immediately by another, as when one sees an object in two perspectives, or **feels it on both sides**. The invariants provide for the detection of **same thing** along with

the detection of **different aspect**. In recognition over a long interval, when encounters with other objects, other places, or other persons have intervened, the attunement of the brain to the **distinguishing features** of the entity must be deeper and stronger than in recognition over a short interval, but the principle need only be extended to cover it."

"**Identification** and **discrimination** develop together in the child as reciprocals."

[Crick, Francis. The Astonishing Hypothesis: The Scientific Search for the Soul. p.36-41]
" '**gestalt**' as 'an organized whole in which each individual part affects every other, the whole being more than the sum of its parts.' In other words, your brain must actively build up these 'wholes' by finding which combination of the parts seems the most likely to correspond to the relevant aspects of the object in the real world, basing its estimates on your previous experience and on the experience of your distant ancestors, which is embedded in your genes. Obviously, what is important is the **interaction** of the parts. The Gestaltists attempted to classify the types of interaction that appeared to be common in the visual system, calling them **laws of perception**. Their laws of grouping included **proximity, similarity, good continuation, and closure**."

"Their **Law of Proximity** stated that we tend to group together things that are close to one another and more distant from other (similar) objects."

"The fact that you see them in vertical lines is because the distance from one dot to its nearest neighbors is shorter in the vertical direction than in the horizontal one. Other experiments show that proximity usually means '**proximity in space**' rather than proximity on the retina."

"Put another way, the brain usually prefers a sensible interpretation to a freak one, meaning that the **interpretation would not be radically altered by a small change of viewpoint**. This may be so because, in the past, while looking at an object, you were often moving through the visual world, so your brain recorded **different aspects of that object as belonging to one thing**."

[Crick, Francis. The Astonishing Hypothesis: The Scientific Search for the Soul. p.50]
"The **perception of motion** by the brain is handled by two main processes, called (somewhat inaccurately) the '**short-range system**' and the 'long-range system.' The former is believed to occur at an earlier stage of processing than the latter. The short-range system does not recognize objects but merely the changes in the patterns of light sensed by the retina and conveyed to the brain. It extracts movement as a 'primitive' without knowing what is moving. In other words, this simple aspect of motion can usefully be regarded as primary sensation. It operates automatically - that is, it is not influenced by attention. It is suspected that the short-range system can segregate figure from ground using movements information and

that it is responsible for the motion after-effect, sometimes called the 'waterfall effect.' (If you gaze at a waterfall for some time and then shift your gaze to the adjacent rocks, they will briefly appear to move upwards.) There is now some doubt about this; it was recently shown that the motion after-effect can be influenced by attention. The **long-range motion system** appears to register the movement of objects. In stead of just registering movement as such, it registers what is moving from one place to another. This can be influenced by attention."

[Crick, Francis. The Astonishing Hypothesis: The Scientific Search for the Soul. p.59-60]
"**Arousal** is a general condition affecting all of one's behavior, as you may notice when you first wake up in the morning. **Attention** implies to psychologists, as William James said, 'withdrawal from some things in order to deal effectively with others."

"Recall that attention is thought to assist at least some forms of awareness. One form of visual attention is eye movement (often assisted by head movements). Because we see more clearly close to our center of gaze, we get more information about an object if we direct our eyes in that direction. We get coarser information (at least about shape) from objects we are not looking at directly. What controls eye movements? Such movements range from **reflex-like responses**, such as those to a sudden movement at some point outside our center of gaze, to **willed eye movements** ('I wonder what he's doing over there'). All forms of attention are likely to have both reflex and willed components."

[Crick, Francis. The Astonishing Hypothesis: The Scientific Search for the Soul. p.68]
"**Consciousness** in general, and visual awareness in particular, obviously incorporate into their processes much that we have already stored in long-term episodic and categorical memories. What concerns us more is **very short term memory**, since it is plausible to argue that if we lost all forms of memory for new events we would not be conscious. However, this essential form of memory need only last a fraction of a second or perhaps a few seconds at most."

[Crick, Francis. The Astonishing Hypothesis: The Scientific Search for the Soul. p.122-123]
"The density of the cones used for daytime vision is very much greater in the **fovea** - approximately at the center of the eye - and so we can see much finer detail there. This is why you **switch your gaze to something of interest** in order to see it more clearly. Conversely, you can sometimes see in the dark more clearly **out of the corner of your eye**, where the retina has many rods. The eye can move in different ways. It can make jumps, called 'saccades,' usually three or four times a second. The eyes of primates can follow a moving object, a process called **'smooth pursuit**.' Curiously, it is almost impossible to

move your eyes smoothly over a stationary scene by just willing to do so. If you try to, it will move in jumps. The eye also makes continual tiny movements of various sorts. If, by one means or another the image on the retina is held completely stationary, it fades from consciousness after a second or two."

[Crick, Francis. The Astonishing Hypothesis: The Scientific Search for the Soul. p.205]

"In his book **Mental Models** he puts this idea in a wider context. He suggests that the division between **conscious** and **unconscious** processes is a result of the very high degree of parallelism in the brain. Such **parallel processing** allows the organism to evolve special sensory, cognitive, and motor systems that operate rapidly, since many of their neurons can work at the same time (rather than one after another) as I have already described for the visual system. The overall control of all this activity by the more serial operating system enables decisions to be made rapidly and flexibly. A very rough analogy would be to an orchestral conductor (the operating system) controlling the parallel activities of all the members of an orchestra. While this operating system can monitor the output of the neural systems it controls, he postulated that it does not have access to the details of their operations but only the results they present to it. By **introspection** we have access to only a limited amount of what is going on in our brains. We have no access to the many operations that lead up to the information given to the brain's operating system. As he puts it, in introspection, 'We tend to force intrinsically parallel notions into a serial straitjacket,' since he envisages the operating system as operating largely in a serial manner. This is why introspection can be so misleading."

[Crick, Francis. The Astonishing Hypothesis: The Scientific Search for the Soul. p.209-210]

"Unfortunately, we don't yet know how the brain expresses this third type of **binding**. What is especially unclear is whether, in **focused awareness**, we are conscious of only one object at a time, or whether our brains can deal with **several objects simultaneously**. We certainly appear to be aware of more than one object at once, but could this be an illusion? Does the brain really deal with several objects one after another in such rapid succession that they appear to be simultaneous? Perhaps we can attend to only one object at a time but, having attended, can **briefly 'remember'** several of them."

[Canter, David. Psychology for Architects. p.37-41]

"**Perceptual Constancy.** To many people it comes as a surprise that the sensations they receive from the world about them are vary varied although their perceptions are relatively stable. For instance, a wall painted white is unlikely to be physically the same colour along its full length, especially if a bright light is shining on it, but we **perceive it of think** it as white wall in all but exceptional circumstances. Similarly, because the retina is essentially two dimensional, a square table will give rise to an image on the retina which is only rarely square. It will vary from diamond to trapezoid depending on our angle of view. Indeed the use of perspective drawing relates to this, but nonetheless we usually **perceive** the table as a square one."

"Besides shape and brightness constancy, we experience colour and size constancy in much the same way. Perceptual constancies are thus an excellent example of the way in which our **knowledge of the world modifies what we perceive**. If we 'know' what an object is, we know and perceive it as the appropriate size, shape, etc. It is a task, requiring some training, to isolate the abstract formal qualities of the object."

"it is our knowledge of what the world is like, built up from previous experience, which creates these **distortions of perception**."

"In general terms, the same can be said of the **perception of space**. In so far as it is understood by present day psychologists, it seems that the perception of space is based, in the main, upon the use of cues that are normally associated with **distance** in our daily life. These cues are the sorts of things which artists use, such as parallax, the difference in gradients of texture with different distances and the apparent convergence of parallel lines. Clearly many of these cues are learnt, together with the possibly subtler cues from bodily sensations such as convergence of the eyes for focusing and the relationships between **what we can see and what we can feel** with our hands."

"there is some evidence to suggest that our perception of space develops very early in life."

"People have a wide range of previous experience to draw upon and thus perception relies upon a variety of sources other than the retina, not least of which is the experience stored in the brain."

"In relation to architecture, at a general level, as Ittelson has pointed out there is much to suggest that there are **environmental constancies** much as there are the types of **object constancies** we have been discussing."

"From the earliest days of psychology it has been clear that a person's **attention span** is severely limited usually to **only about six discrete entities**. This span can be shown in a number of ways, for instance, as the number of random digits which can be remembered over a short period of time or the number of objects that can be accurately identified when presented briefly. One consequence of this is that attention itself plays an important role in perception and needs to be taken account of when considering the design of actual environments."

[Hall, Edward, T. Handbook for Proxemic Research. p.19-21]

"**illusions** are caused by the brain's 'faulty' interpretation of input data (Gardner 1970). This is an excellent example of what is termed a **deficit model** as contrasted with a **context model**, in which the same information but with altered context yields different 'meaning.' The differences between the two interpretations are basic and result in entirely different actions. The deficit model seeks to correct a deficiency which often does not exist. The context model leads the investigator to look more deeply at the structure and relationships of two or more different systems. The deficit model speaks of dietary deficiencies, setting deprivation, the underprivileged, the underdeveloped, the underachievers, understimulation, cultural deprivation, and the substandard or deviant in language and behavior. The context model, on the other hand, is built on the assumption that behavior is primarily adaptive, regardless of how bizarre it appears."

"The **spatial experience** is a transaction, a function of sensory inputs and how they are processed in the brain. The senses are integrated on different levels or in different ways in the brain; first as Gestalts, possibly in the **limbic system**; second, as acknowledged, **identifiable symbols** and signs, ideally with specific **assigned meanings**, in the neocortex."

"The cortical/limbic distinction is basic, and it is important to know, as well as to make explicit, whether one is dealing with, examining, exploring, or discussing the cortical **semeotic level** (Watson 1972a) or the **limbic Gestalt level**. The former is low-context, the latter high-context."

"Over the years I have observed that certain people, even though they have not been caught up in the semiotic web, can, like Goodall's chimpanzees (1971), still put two and two together. This is despite the popular belief that intelligence and verbal facility are synonymous; in other words that man only thinks in symbols. Such people are much more likely to sort out the sensory data in a transaction than individuals who are stuck in semeotics."

"(the further one proceeds toward the semeotic end of the scale) paradoxically the less **'meaning'** one can attach to the event under observation."

[Heider, Fritz. On Perception, Event Structure, and Psychological Environment. p.78-79]

"The question, in what terms should one describe perceptual processes, is put in the form:"

"**Distal determinants**: to 'single out a few aspects of behavioral things and compare them with real ones.' That is to say, one may determine how constant the coordinations between perceptual phenomena and distant objects are."

"**Proximal determinants**: we have to distinguish between (a) local proximal determinants and (b) nonlocal proximal determinants."

"**Local proximal determinants**: we find many cases in which there is no correspondence between the local proximal stimulus and the perceptual phenomenon. For example: 'The constancy of real things is to a great extent preserved in the constancy of the phenomenal things despite variations in their proximal stimuli' "

"The principle of **nonlocal proximal determination** has to be accepted: in such an experiment we would find the perceptual process coordinated only to proximal events, not to objects."

[Downs, R. M. and Stea, D. Image and Environment: Cognitive Mapping and Spatial Behavior. p.4]
"the empirical limits upon cognition, and the 'objective' weighing of alternative decision criteria led to **the principle of bounded rationality**: The capacity of the human mind for formulating and solving complex problems is very small compared with the size of the problems whose solution is required for objectively rational behavior in the real world-or even for a reasonable approximation to such objective rationality. (Simon, 1957, p. 198)   Behavior based on bounded rationality may seem 'irrational' and may be characterized as such, but the resemblance is only apparent. Rather, the essential characteristics of the cognitive process are its limited ability to cope with and store information and its attempt to **form impressions** of and tentative decisions **about the environment** on the basis of limited, fragmentary information under severe time constraints."
"In Simon's boundedly rational model, he satisfices, finding a course of action which is 'good enough' for the situation as he comprehends it."

[Downs, R. M. and Stea, D. Image and Environment: Cognitive Mapping and Spatial Behavior. p.22-23]
"In our studies of cognitive maps, we have overlooked the range and number of sensory modalities through which spatial information is acquired, and have ignored the integrative nature of cognitive processes related to spatial information. The visual, tactile, olfactory, and kinaesthetic sense modalities combine to give an **integrated representation** of any spatial environment. The modalities are complementary despite our intuitive belief (and linguistic bias) that visual information is predominant." "sensory-motor interaction with the spatial environment is necessary for correct perception, for experiencing the world 'as it really is.' "
"information literally floods the person from all of his sensory modes. He must be selective in what he attends to: 'learning by doing.' "

[Craik, K. H. The Comprehension of the Everyday Physical Environment. p. 30]
"In the long run, psychological research should yield an understanding of the manner in which any entity of the everyday **physical environment is comprehended**. The term 'environmental display' will be adopted to signify generally **'that which is comprehended'**- that is, those units of the everyday physical

environment, of which buildings, urban scenes, and forest glades are instances. **Environmental displays** may be considered to vary along at least two important dimensions: scale, and natural to man-influenced. As Figure 1 suggests, a flower would be small scale, natural; a tool, small scale, man-influenced; the Grand Canyon viewed from the air, large scale, natural; and Manhattan Island viewed from the air, large scale, man-influenced."

"The term **'display'** has been chosen because of its flexible application along these continua and because of its connotation of something that is to be reacted to in perceptual-cognitive-affective modalities."

[Craik, K. H. The Comprehension of the Everyday Physical Environment. p. 33-34]
"In studies of **enduring images** of familiar environmental displays, it will be of interest to study the different descriptions given when the environmental display is identified only by name, and when it actually is presented. C. The Nature and Format of Judgments. The kinds of descriptions requested of observers of environmental displays and the format provided for guiding and assisting them in making their responses are of central importance, for they are the signs by which the nature of the observer's comprehensions is made known to us."

[Craik, K. H. The Comprehension of the Everyday Physical Environment. p. 36]
"It would also be possible to explore the degree of association of individual **response** variables with variations in objective, physical characteristics among the sample of displays."

"it might well become possible to predict at the preconstruction stage both how human observers, and even specific subgroups of observers, will most likely **comprehend** the environmental display and how the environmental display will be evaluated in terms of its success in fulfilling its function. The ability of environmental psychology to develop predictive power in this area can be expected to have important effects upon the development and selection of prototypical designs and plans for man-influenced environmental transformations and to place the process of design and planning more directly under rational guidance."

[Collins, John B. Perceptual Dimensions of Architectural Space Validated against Behavioral Criteria. p.6]
"In terms of some adages of design, an operational language (for designers as well as behavioral scientists) must interpret the interaction and the perception of the environment as co-causal factors, that is, one's **reactions to the environment** determines one's perception of the environment. Conversely, the **perception of the environment** greatly affects one's reaction to it."

[Rapoport, Amos. History and Precedent in Environmental Design. p. 282]

"Generally, the higher the **speed** the less **information** per unit length is needed in the environment. There are clearly also differences between a scenic road and a freeway because context will modify even high-speed movement."

"In general, pedestrian rarely look above eye level in enclosed urban spaces; thus the **perception** of detail becomes inevitable, and this becomes what such settings require. Given the needs of drivers as described, their movement channels should be simple."

[Hay, D. R. Proportion, or the Geometric Principle of Beauty, Analyzed. p.8-9]

"Although I have hitherto referred to the effects of forms upon one eye only, in order to be more explicit, these effects are much modified by the rays entering both our eyes simultaneously; hence the **mild and pleasing influence** of horizontal composition, and the **more powerful and grand impression** made by that which is vertical. These are the sensible effects of figure upon the organs of vision, and it is only of such that I mean to treat. My observation can therefore have no reference to any geometrical property in figures beyond what can be superficially depicted, as they are reflected upon the retina; for it is well known that we only find out by experience that bodies possess other dimensions than what may be thus appreciated. The effects of geometrical configuration on the eye are, in the first instance, regulated by the relation they bear to the conformation of that organ itself; hence the **soft influence** of those of the curved kind, and the acute and **more powerful** effect of those whose outlines are composed of angles. On the mode of proportioning these elements of form in the combinations of various figures, their effect upon the eye depends- when a proper mode is adopted, geometric beauty is the result, while the adoption of an improper mode results in deformity."

[Wilson, Colin St. John. The Natural Imagination: An Essay on the Experience of Architecture. p.65-69]

"**Kant's** statement that 'all our consciousness is grounded in spatial experience.' From the moment of being born we spend our lives in a state of comfort or discomfort on a scale of sensibility that stretches between claustrophobia and agoraphobia. We are **inside** or **outside** or on the **threshold** between. There are no other places to be."

"From Melanie Klein's work on infant psychology Stokes takes the concept of two polar **'positions'** or modes of experience through which (it is claimed) we all pass in infancy and against which all our subsequent experience in life is re-enacted. (That the word 'position' with all its connotations of physical space, presence and stance, was chosen to define a psychological state goes a very long way to meet the case that I shall be putting forward.) The first 'position' is identified as an all-embracing **envelopment** with the mother, of one-ness: what Freud called 'the oceanic feeling', a kind of fusion which is most sheltering. This form of attachment is grounded in an intimate experience of the protective and sustaining qualities of the mother-figure which at this stage is largely received as an unfocused, all-enveloping environment in a kind of emotional and aesthetic short-sight. By definition the nature of this mode of Envelopment is spatial, physical tactile. There is a close analogue to this 'position' in the architectural experience of interior space that is modelled in rhythmic forms of flowing and merging continuity. It is argued that this position of Envelopment is succeeded by a fundamental and shocking change to the contrary position of **Exposure or Detachment**- of an otherness in which the infant becomes aware both of its own separate identity from the mother and from all other objects out there. This experience is the beginning of objectivity and self-sufficiency. The architectural analogue for the 'position' of independence lies in the experience of open space and the external confrontation with a building's wholeness and self-sufficiency, the carved and massive frontality of its stance over-against you."

"It is presumably therefore not unreasonable to assume, in conventional psycho-analytical terms, that those manifest forms carry a significant charge of latent subject matter. I think that it is to this tension below the aesthetic surface that Stokes alludes when he talks about the paintings of Piero and Cezanne in terms of 'the **image in form**' as distinct from 'the imaginary of the subject-matter'."

" '**Formal relationships** themselves entails a representation of imagery of their own though these likenesses are not as explicit as the image we obtain from what we call the subject matter.' Form itself takes on the property of being a code and thereby becomes deep content: in architecture as in painting. And what stirs most deeply in the latent imagery of architectural forms is the memory of the **human body**."

"The code acts so directly and vividly upon us because it is strangely familiar. It is in fact the first language we ever learned, long before words; for it is that body of sensations and appetites and responses experienced by the infant in passing through the two polar 'positions'. Such body-images must have been the only metaphors available to the infant in its projection of fantasies and from this conjunction must have gained a yet greater emotional charge. It is a language drawn from a wide range of **sensual and spatial experience**. But then it is intrinsically these sensations that are the primary vehicle for architectural experience."

"In his pursuit of the body metaphor Stokes is careful to disclaim any attempt 'to anthropomorphise building in a literal sense. It would be indeed destructive to the architectural significance.' Instead he is concerned to elicit 'the feel of a body surviving in a remote transposition' in 'which architectural forms are a language confined to the joining of a few ideographs of immense ramification."

"Architecture offers a whole typology of counterforms to the 'positions' experienced in this body language. Louis Kahn once said that 'certain forms imply certain functions and certain functions call for certain forms.' "

"It is indicative of the primacy of these counterforms that they preempt all considerations of structure...and all discriminations of style."

"The primary forms of **envelopment** are room and roof; both have a clear identity to which specific qualities of 'position' can be assigned."

"The opposite condition - **exposure** - is experienced not only in the extreme form of agoraphobia (in which the lack of protective boundary can lead to panic) but also in the drama of confrontation that can take place between the facade of a monumental building and the visitor who, approaching across open space, is compelled to stand of a respectful distance and, in that intuitive act of deference, is make to feel vulnerable. Buildings vary in the degree of assertion with which they confront the visitor: this is in proportion not only to sheer size but also to the degree of frontality."

"Next the **threshold** - a defined place betwixt and between, a moderating pause to acclimatize oneself to the difference between inside and outside. ...the in-between quality of the threshold, partaking equally of both outdoorness and enclosure."

[Pearson, David. Making Sense of Architecture. p.70]

" 'When you are in a healing environment, you know it; no analysis is required. **You somehow feel** welcome, balanced, and at one with yourself and the world. You are both relaxed and stimulated, reassured...you feel at home.' But if we feel this healing essence of the place, what components go into creating its effect? Much of it is to do with **heightening personal awareness** of components that influence health and carefully combining qualities of physical, mental and emotional."

"Our surroundings, he feels, can **desensitize** us morally and socially or support the inner processes of growth that are the foundation of health; they can contribute to stress and general malaise or balance and strengthen our attitude to life."

"Nothing is new and **architecture that appeals to the senses and is healing** has ancient roots. Spas, shrines and the erotic seraglios were all variations of the central need for a fully sensory and sensual environment. The Greeks built a network of rural healing temples called 'aesculapia': near the sea, oriented to the sun and fresh prevailing breezes and in harmony with their natural setting, they could be a model for today."

"Free forms and spaces, daylight, harmonious colours, the sound of cascading water, light through stained glass, the scent of growing plants, combine with fresh air from natural ventilation, solar design, and energy-conserving systems to create an architecture that honors the senses."

APPENDIX C: ' MODEL-CLOUD '

[Stea, D. Space, Territory and Human Movement. p.14]

"Our major interest is in territorial changes and their effects, but change cannot be asserted without defining the situation that existed before the change.   A variety of techniques exists for asserting contributory aspects of behavior."

"The individual, it may be assumed, also possesses a **mental map** or **environmental image** of the space represented by the cluster; using techniques similar to those employed by Kevin Lynch in his investigation of the conceptual form of cities, we can determine the perceived nature of units, clusters and complexes, and of the paths connecting them."

[Downs, R. M. and Stea, D. Image and Environment: Cognitive Mapping and Spatial Behavior. p.9]

"Underlying our definition is a view of behavior which, although variously expressed, can be reduced to the statement that 'human spatial behavior is dependent on the individual's **cognitive map of the spatial environment'**. That this formulation is necessary is indicated by a comparison of the characteristics of the individual with those of the spatial environment.

The environment is a large-scale surface, complex in both the categories of information present and in the number of instances of each category. Things are neither uniformly distributed over this surface, nor ubiquitous: they have a 'whereness' quality. In contrast, the individual is a relatively small organism with limited mobility, stimulus-sensing capabilities, information processing ability, storage capacity, and available time. The individual receives information from a complex, uncertain, changing, and unpredictable source via a series of imperfect sensory modalities operating over varying time spans and intervals between time spans. From such diversity the individual must aggregate information to form a **comprehensive representation of the environment**. This process of acquisition, amalgamation, and storage is cognitive mapping, and the product of this process at any point in time can be considered as a **cognitive map**.

Given a cognitive map, the individual can formulate the basis for a strategy of environmental behavior. We view cognitive mapping as a basic component in human adaptation, and the cognitive map as a requisite both for human survival and for everyday environmental behavior. It is a coping mechanism through which the individual answers two basic questions quickly and efficiently: (1) Where certain valued things are; (2) How to get to where they are from where he is."

[Ittelson, William H. and Proshansky, Harold M. An Introduction to Environmental Psychology: Research Methods in Environmental Psychology. p.236-237]

"conceptualizing the global environment in terms of its **images**, or molar map of an area that everyone carries around in his mind. As a research method cognitive mapping can reveal something about how people use their environment (in the sense of finding their way around in it) as well as what it means to them symbolically. It derives from the fact that it is impossible to perceive, say, the city of Boston, Massachusetts, or Middlesex County, New Jersey. One can experience only that part of it within his immediate range of perception at any given moment. As a result we 'visualize' what we cannot perceive. Everyone carries many such **'imaged' models** in his mind simultaneously. At the same time these cognitive maps are almost never replicas of the actual land- or city-scape; rather, they arise from useful distortions of the environment based on previous experiences with it."

"it deals with how the inhabitants of cities read the physical world as a **'generalized mental picture.'** (Lynch 1960) In this sense it provides an additional research perspective to our study of cities, limiting its concern to the immediate physical environment and the ways in which it is ordered cognitively."

[Gibson, J.J. The Senses Considered as Perceptual Systems. p.112-113]

"The question to be answered is this: How does a perceiver feel what he is touching instead of the cutaneous impressions and the bone postures as such? The animal registers the shape of the enclosure in which he is hidden; the man registers the shape of the chair in which he sits."

"The question involves the perceiving of both the general layout of environmental surfaces and the particular layout of the surfaces of an object being manipulated. How is the arrangement or shape of these surfaces detected? The question is clearly related to that of so-called space perception. I have argued that the perception of the layout of surfaces is the perception of space."

"This is the space to which an individual is oriented, with respect to which the posture and equilibrium of his body is maintained."

"but it is not really a space. The body percept, or 'body image,' is a set of possible dispositions or poses-standing, or lying-relative to the substratum and to gravity. If it is a space at all, it is subjective rather than objective. And it is fluid instead of rigid, for it can adopt any of a vast family of poses by moving from one to another."

"Now to answer the question. In brief, the suggestion is that the joints yield **geometrical information**, that the skin yields **contact information**, and that in certain invariant combinations they yield **information specifying the layout of external surfaces**. At any one moment the orchestrated input from the joints (the evidence for this will be given later) specifies a set of bone directions relative to the spine, to the head, and to the direction of gravity. The bones and the extremities are thus linked to the environment. At any one moment, the total input from the skin likewise specifies a pattern of contacts with touching surfaces, one of which is always the surface of support. The skin is thus also connected to the environment by this simultaneous pattern."

"What about dimensions and distances in haptic space as contrasted with directions? Some evidence exists. The space between the opposable thumb and the index finger (or any other finger) is clearly experienced. This use of the hand is like that of the mandible in an insect (Katz and MacLeod, 1949). With eyes closed one can measure of the diameters of familiar coins with some success (cf. Kelvin, 1954). The width of two blocks can be compared successively in this way, and small differences can be detected. Or the width and height of the same object can be compared by successive spanning with two finger. In fact, the relative spans between all five fingers, as we shall see. Note that when five fingers all touch an object, there are five distinct sensations of touch but there is a **perception of only one object**. This fact will be elaborated later. Multiple touching of this sort yields haptic perception in the literal meaning of **'laying hold of'**.

[Crick, Francis. The Astonishing Hypothesis: The Scientific Search for the Soul. p. 32-33]

"what we expect to find in the brain is a representation of the visual scene in some symbolic form. Well, you might say, why should there not be a symbolic screen in the brain. Suppose the screen were made of an ordered array of nerve cells. Each nerve cell would handle the activity at one particular 'point' in the picture. the activity of the cell would be proportional to the intensity of the light at that point. If there were a lot of light there, that nerve cell would be very active; if no light, then it would be inactive. (By having a set of three nerve cells for each point we could deal with color as well.) Thus the representation would be symbolic. The cells of this postulated screen do not produce light, but some form of electrical activity that symbolizes light. Why should this not be all we need? The trouble with such an arrangement is that it would not be 'perceiving' anything except little individual patches of light. It could not see, any more than your television set can see. You can tell a friend: 'Let me know when that nice young woman starts reading the news,' but it is no use trying to wire up your television set to do this. It has no way built into it for recognizing a woman, let alone a particular one performing a particular action.yet your brain (or your friend's brain) can do this with little or no apparent effort. So the brain cannot get by with just sets of cells that merely show what sort of light intensity is where. It must produce a symbolic description at a higher level, probably at a series of higher levels. As we have seen, this is not a straightforward matter, since it must find the best interpretation of the visual signals given its past experience. Thus, what the brain has to build up is a many-levelled interpretation of the visual scene, usually in terms of objects and events and their meaning to us. As an object, like a face, is often made up of parts (such as eyes, nose, mouth, etc.) and those parts of subparts, so this symbolic interpretation is likely to occur at several levels."

"The brain must make those interpretations explicit. An explicit representation of something is what is symbolized there without further extensive processing."

"In neural terms, 'explicit' probably means that nerve cells must be firing in a way that symbolizes such information fairly directly. Thus it is plausible that we need an explicit multilevel, symbolic **interpretation of the visual scene** in order to 'see' it. It is difficult for many people to accept that what they see is a symbolic interpretation of the world-it all seems so like 'the real thing.' But in fact we have no direct knowledge of objects in the world. This is an illusion produced by the very efficiency of the system since, as we have seen, our interpretations can occasionally be wrong. Instead, people often prefer to believe that there is a disembodied soul that, in some utterly mysterious way, does the actual seeing, helped by the elaborate apparatus of the brain. Such people are called 'dualists'- they believe that matter is one thing and mind is something completely different. Our Astonishing Hypothesis says, on the contrary, that this is not the case, that it's all done by nerve cells. What we are considering is how to decide between these two views experimentally."

[Crick, Francis. The Astonishing Hypothesis: The Scientific Search for the Soul. p. 53]
"I shall mention only in passing certain other visual constancies. An object looks roughly the same even if we so not look at it directly, so that it falls on a different part of the retina. We recognize it as the same object even when we see it at another distance, so that the size of its image on the retina is larger or smaller, or even if it is rotated somewhat. We take these different constancies somewhat for granted, but a simple vision machine would not be able to perform such feats unless it had built-in devices for doing so, as the developed brain must have. Exactly how the brain does all this is still somewhat uncertain."

[Crick, Francis. The Astonishing Hypothesis: The Scientific Search for the Soul. p. 206-207]
"humans directly experience only the presented side of objects in the visual field; the presence of the invisible rear of an object is only an inference. On the other hand, he believes that **visual understanding**-what one is aware of- is determined by the **3D model** together with 'conceptual structures'- fancy words for thoughts. This illustrates what he means by the intermediate-level theory of consciousness."

"An example may make this clearer. If you look at a person whose back is turned to you, you can see the back of his head but not his face. Nevertheless, your brain infers that he has a face. We can deduce this because if he turned around and showed that the front of his head has no face, you would be very surprised. The viewer-centerd representation corresponds to what you saw of the back of his head. It is what you are vividly aware of. What your brain infers about the front would come from some sort of 3D model representation. Jackendoff believes you are not directly conscious of this 3D model (nor of your thoughts, for that matter). Recall the old line: How do I know what I think till I hear what I say."

"When you imagine the front of the face in the example above, what you are aware of is a conscious surface representation generated by the unconscious 3D model. This distinction between the two types of representation will probably have to be refined as the subject develops, but it gives us a rough first idea of what it is we are trying to explain."

APPENDIX D: PROXEMICS

[Hall, Edward T. Handbook for Proxemic Research. p.2-3]

"The study of culture in the **proxemic sense** is the study of people's use of their perceptual apparatus in different emotional states during different activities, in different relationships, settings, and contexts. No single research technique is sufficient in scope to investigate this complex multi-dimensional subject. The research technique is, therefore, a function of the particular facet under examination at the time and may call for the involvement of many disciplines. **Proxemics**, as I think of it, is more concerned with how than why, and more with form than content. The work is admittedly detailed and is apt at times to be dull and repetitious. To complicate matters, **proxemics** addresses itself to basic human situations in an area of culture that is ordinarily hidden from conscious awareness. For this reason, given the deeply interrelated nature of culture, **proxemics frequently** leads to new insights about specific cultures, as well as to insights into the generalized concept of culture itself. My thinking concerning **proxemics** is based on the assumption that all culture is ultimately an extension of basic biological processes. While man's extensions, as they evolve, may mask the underlying relationships which maintain the equilibrium of biological systems, the relationships and systems are no less real by virtue of being hidden. **Proxemics** is the study of man's transactions as he perceives and uses intimate, personal, social, and public space ' in various setting while following out-of-awareness dictates of cultural paradigms."

"Any culture characteristically produces a simultaneous array of patterned behavior on several different levels of awareness. It is therefore important to specify which levels of awareness one is dealing with. **Proxemic Patterns**, once learned, are maintained largely outside conscious awareness, and thus have to be investigated without probing the conscious minds of one's subjects. Direct questioning will yield few if any of the significant insights."

[Hall, Edward T. Handbook for Proxemic Research. p.5]

"man shares with other forms of life a discrete set of distances (**proxemic zones**) which he maintains from his fellow men (Hall 1966). For non-contact Americans these are: intimate distance, personal distance, social-consultative distance, and public distance. Which zone is occupied at any given moment in the course of an encounter is a function of at least three sets of variables: the **transaction**, the relationship of the two persons in social system, and the feeling or emotions of both parties."

[Hall, Edward T. Handbook for Proxemic Research. p.16-18]

"the degree to which people are emotionally involved with each other is reflected in the way they use and structure space and vice versa. Not only are there spaces that pull people together (sociopetal) but even ways of arranging furniture that reduce involvement (**sociofugal**). Two examples at opposite ends of the involvement scale would be the north Germans and the Italians (Hall 1966).

"the investigator needs to know **sensory involvement** over time."

"By sensory involvement one means: to what degree is it possible to hear, see, smell, or feel the vibrations of movement of other human beings which are either pleasant or annoying or even bothersome and stressful. In India, for example, there is a very high level of auditory involvement at any time of the day or night, which apparently is not stressful to most Indians but frequently drives Americans to distractions."

"Everything that is known from proxemic research points to the fact that instead of something that can be summarized in feet and inches one is dealing with a kind of language involving all the senses as measured by the 19 proxemic scales."

[Hall, Edward T. Handbook for Proxemic Research. p.21]

"**Proxemics** is, by and large, a high-context field with all that that implies. The methods of gathering, analyzing, and presenting proxemic data appear to be different in degree than for language, although proxemics performs many functions comparable to language (Hall 1936b). The mere fact that all the senses are involved in distance setting means that any statement must take this fact into account. We would therefore expect to find somewhat more leeway in proxemic systems than in language. Furthermore, if proxemics is treated as though it were an information or a content science rather than a context science, the results will be ambiguous at best. The study of proxemics is best accomplished in what will be termed situational frames and as a function of action chains in these frames. It is only in situational frames that it is possible to control both information and context."

"**Proxemics**, like kinesics and language, deals with moving, structured events. This means or implies at least passing familiarity with two basic processes, (1) action chains and (2) situational frames,"

"The proxemicist ultimately has to deal with the idiosyncratic in the sense that he must transcend it, because he is not as concerned with **individual differences** as much as he is with identifying the basic **group pattern** that can be counted on to signal shifts in context."

"**Proxemics** is a synthesizing, contexting science. Like language, it reflects and is reflected in the entirety of culture. Little happens or is thought of that does not occur in a temporal and spatial frame, and that frame provides much of the context in which events occur, albeit an unspoken or taken-for-granted frame. Like culture in general, proxemics is inclusive, so it is important to have some means for being explicit - a frame of reference in which to context the research. Three concepts are necessary to achieve this goal: (a) Relationship of context to meaning; (b) Action chains, which occur in (c) Situational frames."

"**High-Context** (H/C) situations are characterized by a minimal flow of information (1) and therefore either great speed of transmission or very small channels. **Low-context** (L/C) situations are the reverse. H/C situations are quite stable and require considerable time in which to build the context either into the culture over time or into the memory drums of individuals within the culture. Nonverbal systems are high on the context scale - much higher - than symbolic systems. For example, time and space, as a rule, perform important contexting functions. It also follows that H/C cultures would attach more importance to those cultural systems, such as proxemics, that are concerned with or perform contexting functions. L/C cultures, on the other hand, will tend to minimize or to selectively disregard the contexting aspects of culture while attaching more importance to those systems that are concerned with information."

[Hall, Edward T. Handbook for Proxemic Research. p.28]
"Distance between the interviewer seated behind the desk and the subject across from him should be 'comfortable talking distance.' **This will vary with the room shape, ceiling height, and emotional state of the subject**. In all cases, the subject should be permitted to move his chair to where he feels

comfortable if he shows an inclination to do so. The whole matter of position during interviews is highly critical and radically affects the results."

[Hall, Edward T. Handbook for Proxemic Research. p.38]

"The **Proxetic Notation (PN) system** deals specifically with the recording of how people use their senses in interpersonal encounters. Under ideal conditions it permits the objective (etic) transcription of sensory involvement in interactions. **Proxetic events** are the physically different events as defined in the PN system, while **proxemes** are the psychologically different, culturally patterned perceptions of those events."

"The MAIN purpose of PN, then, is to provide a tool for pinpointing and recording **proxetic units of behavior**. A simultaneous result achieved is the added awareness of any investigator trained in PN to recognize and distinguish between different modes of non-verbal communication."

[Canter, David. Psychology for Architects. p.113]

"Beyond these observations of people in public places relatively little study has been carried out of **the way in which people relate themselves to physical objects in a wide range of situation**. This is a pity because it is clear that people do not make use of their physical surroundings in a random way. Indeed much of architecture assumes that quite definite patterns will occur. For instance, it is often assumed that a particular furniture arrangement will be used in rooms and they are designed with this in mind. Many architects are surprised to find that the arrangements which seem obvious to them do not actually occur. One reason why so little study has been made of the relationships which people take up vis-a-vis their physical surroundings is the observation that much of human spatial behaviour is more readily explained in terms of the relationships people take up in respect to other people. The observations of waiting behaviour or of seat selection in a restaurant could well be re-interpreted in terms of people using the physical environment to enable them to locate themselves in a desired position with respect to the activities of others rather than simply their physical surroundings. However, it must not be forgotten that there clearly are cases in which **people do deal with physical entities** seemingly **independently of their social implications**. One example that I have noted frequently is the fact that people waiting near bus stops in Glasgow tend to stand slightly further away from the bus stop itself than they do from one another. Informal observations suggest that while the mean distance between people is a little over two feet the mean distance people stand from the bus stop is nearer to three feet."

[Canter, David. Psychology for Architects. p.121-123]

"the relationships between patterns of human behaviour and the architectural configurations within which that behaviour takes place."

"the use of space may be considered both as determined by the people and a determiner of human behaviour. But what can we say about its role? We have seen that a simple and direct extrapolation from animal behaviour is not tenable and so we must look to other propositions which take account of uniquely human qualities, whilst still drawing upon the central principles underlying animal use of space. One possibility is that we use space as yet another medium of communication, that we use it **to indicate our feelings** of, or attitudes towards, the type of activity in which we intend to engage. In an experiment carried out by Porter et al. specifically to test this possibility with regard to **interpersonal proximity** it was not possible to show that anything was communicated at all. Thus the fact that we may be able to interpret intentions or feelings from the use of space in some situation (as Little, for instance, has shown) does not necessarily mean that we actively use space as a means of expression. A different view comes from looking at the work initiated by Festinger and his colleagues. In those studies **a person's location influenced the information he received**, the people he met and hence the friendships he made. If we accept that information is not spread evenly over the environment then the location a person is in will influence his relationship to that information. The Festinger studies showed this to be the case at the scale of building layouts. Does this interpretation make sense at the level of the smaller scale of the position of people in rooms? Certainly the relationship between **eye contact** and **distance** indicates the greater the distance between people the greater the amount of information they try to obtain by looking. It is also possible to interpret the various studies by Sommer as indicating that people arrange themselves in various positions in order **to minimise or optimise the amount of information they receive from others**. The patterns found in the studies, the places people locate themselves in space, also fits in with this information hypothesis. It fits provided we regard it as information balance, **control over interaction, that people are trying to achieve** when locating themselves at the periphery in restaurants, say, or near to pillars in public waiting places. Accepting then that one of the major roles of human spatial behaviour is to control the quantities and quality of interaction in which a person will take part, what are the general implications for design? One important implication comes from dismissing the analogy with animals. When designers accept this analogy there is a tendency for them to cast the users of their buildings in a subordinate role, as of a dog to its master. There is a tendency for them to assume that they know the hidden, innate forces which determine what people do and that they can thus manipulate these forces without the users being aware or being able to respond any differently than the designer wishes. Casting the user in an active role, trying to find a situation which optimises the balance between the communications, or information, which he wants to receive and which he wants to give, forces the designer to think more carefully about the people who will be using his building. **Why they will be there**."

[Johnson, Susan and Marano, Hara Estroff. Attachment: The Immutable Longing for Contact. p.36]
" 'The expression of emotion is the primary communication system in relationships; it's how we adjust to **closeness and distance**.' "
"We seek close physical proximity to a partner, and rely on their continuing affections and availability, because it is a survival need. What satisfies the need for attachment in adults is what satisfies the need in the young: Eye contact, touching, stroking, and holding a partner deliver the same security and comfort. When threatened, or fearful, or experiencing loss, we turn to our partner for psychological comfort."

[Craik, K. H. The Comprehension of the Everyday Physical Environment. p.34]
"many **reactions to the nonhuman environment** are subtle and are neither customarily nor easily talked about in everyday discourse. These procedures, therefore, entail unusual modes of responding to environmental displays. If the **subtlety of reactions to the everyday physical surroundings** has been one factor in hampering the development of behavioral science research in this area, as it indeed should be able to make a contribution. Responses are, after all, the business of the psychologist."

[Alexander, Christopher. A Pattern Language: Towns, Buildings, Construction. p.887]
"Our experience has led us to an even stronger version of this pattern - which constrains the shape of ceilings too. Specifically, we believe that people feel uncomfortable in spaces like these: Rooms whose ceilings can make you uncomfortable. We can only speculate on the possible **reason for these feelings**. It seems just possible that they originate from some kind of **desire for a person to be surrounded by** a spherical bubble roughly **related to** the human axis. Room shapes which are more or less versions of this bubble are comfortable; while those which depart from it strongly are uncomfortable. Perhaps when the space around us is too sharply different from the imaginary social bubble around us, we do not feel quite like persons. A ceiling that is flat, vaulted in one direction or vaulted in two directions, has the necessary character. A ceiling sloping to one side does not. We must emphasize that this conjecture is not intended as an argument in favor of rigidly simple or symmetric spaces. It only speaks against those rather abnormal spaces with one-sided sloping ceilings, high apexed ceilings, weird bulges into the room, and re-entrant angles in the wall."

[Thiel, P. Notes on the Description, Scaling, Notation and Scoring of Some Perceptual and Cognitive Attributes of the Physical Environment. p.601]

"Gibson (1947) divides the range of everyday **space experience** into two groups: aerial space and local space. He describes these as follows: **'Aerial space** may be defined as the visual surroundings extending away from the observer and bounded in any direction by the horizon, the surface of the earth and the sky. It may be distinguished from local space primarily by its voluminousness and long range of distances. **Local space** is the kind to which we are accustomed; it is enclosed by walls and restricted in range by them. Even out of doors in a civilized environment the spatial scene is cut up and confined to localized areas by buildings and other objects which obliterate the horizon...' He also points out that 'persons who are adapted to going about and making the ordinary judgements of distance in the city are usually misled by the extent of distances in the desert, mountains, on water or from a plane. Generally, aerial distances are poorly estimated by such persons because they are unfamiliar with the visual cues present in the situation for space perception...' In view of the difficulty of estimating distances accurately, especially larger distances, it is advantageous to have a means of denoting a dimension by bracketing it within a range with an upper and a lower limit. Such a system should possess narrow limits for the smaller, more easily estimated distances, and wider limits as the distances grow larger and more difficult to estimate precisely. As a matter of convenience **a series of zones**, identified 0, 1, 2,...10 may be suggested, with the range limits for each zone as in the accompanying table. These range dimensions are derived from a logarithmic scale based on points at 6 feet and 15,000 feet. The average ratio between successive dimensions is about 2.4. (The dimensions have been rounded off to the nearest whole number.)"

"6 ft. is a minimum dimension for a **habitable space**. 7-12 ft. is a distant phase of social-consultative distance (Hall, 1963). 40 ft. is the limit for **discerning facial expression** (Spreiregan, 1965). Far phase of **public distance** begins near 30 ft. (Hall, 1963). 80 ft. is the limit for facial recognition (Spreiregan, 1965).

Medieval city squares average 190 x 465 ft. (Sitte, 1945). 450 ft. is the **limit for discerning action** (Spreiregan, 1965). Maximum distance, for **seeing people** is 4,000 ft. (Spreiregan, 1965). 15,000 ft. is **horizon distance** for 5 1/2 ft. eye height (U.S.H.O. Pub. 111B)."

[Heider, Fritz. On Perception, Event Structure, and Psychological Environment. p.69-70]

"Of primary importance for all theories is the question whether distal or proximal data are used as the focus in the determination. One can treat perception and action either in terms of the **distant object** (perception functions in such a way that the distant object is 'attained'; the organism moves toward the food, etc.); or one can treat it in terms of **proximal influences** and effects, that is to say, in terms of processes close to the skin, stimuli, muscle contractions or movements of the limbs."

"These theories fall into two groups. One group stresses perception; to it belong the older theories of perception which emphasized the stimulus-oriented sensations. The other group tests the psychological processes more from the point of view of action and motor phenomena; to it belong the stimulus-response theories. It is easy to see that these theories get their vitality from the general tendency to use proximal determinants and not from observation; observation favors distal determinants much more. The exponents of these theories want to relate psychological processes to the actual concrete influences **which organism and environment exert on each other**. The most important arguments against these theories can be reduced to a single point: observation shows that often distal determination is possible where proximal determination is impossible. Von Kries, Becher, Ehrenfels, and the Gestalt theory used this argument against the older theories of perception; different teleological systems (McDougall, etc.) used this argument against stimulus-response theories. Indeed, the most important problem for all theories using proximal determinants is to show that it is possible to establish that system of determination as the independent one, and further that it is possible to derive from that system the existence of relevant distal determinants, which are found in observation, and to treat them as only apparently relevant determinants. The device which is almost exclusively used for this derivation is selection. There is the infinite number of possibilities of bonds of association or conditioned reflexes between any stimuli and any response. **Contact with the environment establishes or strengthens only a limited, selected number of these bonds**. Selection works in such a way that distal determination, that is to say, correspondence to the objects of the environment, is brought about. However, very often the derivation of distal from proximal determination is effected by the surreptitious substitution of distal for proximal terms."

[Heider, Fritz. On Perception, Event Structure, and Psychological Environment. p.77-78]

"The theory of tropism, as it is presented by Crozier and Hoagland (1934), coordinates 'stimuli' with 'orientation,' that is to say, direction which is determined in relation to the environmental space. Not what is closest to the skin-muscle contractions or movements of the limbs is taken as the focus, but an effect, an achievement of the movement of the limbs. Thus this theory goes a step beyond pure proximal determination. **Determination by orientation** lies between determination by the movements of the organs and distal determination in terms of the objects of the environment. From the following quotations it will be clear that the authors distinguish sharply between proximal determination and determination in terms of orientation, and that they do not think that the second can be reduced to the first. Since the anatomical basis for such actions is quite different in diverse organisms, but the behavior element dynamically identical, it is clear that the quantitative formulations arrived at refer to the behavior, and not to specific accidents of structure...(Crozier and Hoagland, 1934, p.6). The 'anatomical basis' and 'accidents of structure' are proximally determined entities; the 'dynamically identical behavior element' refers to orientation."

[Downs, R. M. and Stea, D. Image and Environment: Cognitive Mapping and Spatial Behavior. p.16-20]
"Locational information is designed to answer the question, Where are these phenomena? and leads to **a subjective geometry of space**. There are two major components to this geometry, distance and direction. Distance can be measured in a variety of ways, and we are surprisingly sensitive to distance in our everyday behavior. The claim that 'it takes you only half an hour to go and get it' will perhaps receive the reply that 'it's too far to go.' We think of distance in terms of time cost, money cost, and the more traditional measures, kilometers and miles. Knowledge of distance - **the amount of separation between pairs of places and pairs of phenomena** - is essential for planning any strategy of spatial behavior. Geography, for example, has developed a series of models of human spatial behavior which depend upon the individual's sensitivity to distance variations and upon his assumed goal of minimizing the distance traveled either by himself or by his products. Direction is no less important in the geometry of space, although **we are less conscious of directional information**. We take direction more for granted than we perhaps should. It is only when we cannot find a map in the glove compartment of the car and become lost that the need for directional information becomes acute. The person who 'gives' directions by pointing vaguely and saying 'it's over there' is no more helpful than one who says 'it's on the left' - we need to know whose left. By combining distance and direction we can arrive at locational information about phenomena."

"Thus, locational information is not as simple as it might appear. We must store many bits of distance and direction data to operate efficiently in a spatial environment, a process involving relatively accurate encoding, storage, and decoding. Use of locational information in formulating a strategy of spatial behavior, however, requires a second type of information: that concerning the attributes of phenomena. Attributive information tells us what kinds of phenomena are 'out there,' and is complementary to locational information, indicating what is at a particular location and **why anybody would want to go there**. An attribute is derived from a characteristic pattern of stimulation regularly associated with a particular phenomenon which, in combination with other attributes, signals **the presence of the phenomenon**. A concrete example will clarify this definition. Imagine that at the end of the search process specified in the drive-in theater example you are confronted with something that you 'recognize' consisting of a large open space surrounded by a wall with an enormous screen at its far end, a small building at a break in the wall, and lots of teenagers driving in and out in cars. Obviously, it is the drive-in movie theater that you were searching for, and the screen and teenagers can be considered attributes of the phenomenon 'movie theater.' You can interpret the **pattern of stimulation (visual in this instance)** as indicating a series of attributes that, in this combination, signal the presence of a drive-in theater. We can divide attributes of phenomena into two major classes: (1) descriptive, quasi-objective, or denotative; and (2) evaluative or connotative. The attributes listed as signaling the presence of the drive-in all belong to the first type, while attributes such as 'reasonable prices,' 'good shows,' or 'easy to get in' are **evaluative or connotative**. Here, we are separating attributes which are affectively neutral (descriptive) from those which are affectively charged (evaluative). This process of evaluation involves a **relationship between a phenomenon and its potential role in the behavior of the experiencing individual**. What is the relationship between an attribute and an object? An object is identified and defined by a set of attributes and bits of locational information. However, what is an object at one spatial scale can become an attribute at another."

"By the distortion of cognitive maps, we mean the cognitive transformations of both distance and direction, such that an individual's **subjective geometry** deviates from the Euclidean view of the real world. Such deviations can have major effects upon the patterns of spatial use of the environment. In terms of the distance distortions, Lee (1962; 1970) has indicated that, given two urban facilities equidistant from an urban resident, one located on the downtown side is considered closer than the one which is away from the city center. If people are sensitive to distance, consequent sp**atial behavior patterns will be dependent** upon such distance distortions. Far more significant, and as yet little understood, are the results of schematization. By schematization we mean the use of cognitive categories into which we **code environmental information and by which we interpret such information**. We are, as Carr (1970, p. 518) suggests, victims of conventionality. This conventionality may be expressed in two ways. The first involves the use of those spatial symbols to which we all subscribe and which we use both as denotative and connotative shorthand ways of coping with the spatial environment. Thus, we all understand (or think we understand) the intended, value-loaded meanings of 'Africa the Dark Continent,' 'Europe the Center of Culture,' 'Behind the Iron Curtain,' and 'The Midwest as the Heartland.' Symbols (often mythological), such as the Western route to India and the search for the Northwest Passage, have had major effects upon the course of history. In general, such symbols deal with large spatial areas and are subscribed to by a large part of the population."

"A second aspect of schematization or conventionality involves the very limited set of cognitive categories or concepts that we have developed in order **to cope with information derived from the spatial environment**. As we were recently told, 'once you've seen one slum, you've seen them all.' Are all older center-city areas 'slums' to middle-class whites or do they have more sophisticated cognitive categories? Our understanding of the semantics (or vocabulary) of cognitive maps is remarkably limited."

APPENDIX E: PRIMORDIAL NEED: SECURITY

[Johnson, Susan and Marano, Hara Estroff. Attachment: The Immutable Longing for Contact. p.34]

"The need for physical closeness between a mother and child serves evolutionary goals; in a dangerous world, a responsive caregiver ensures survival of an infant.   Attachment Theory states that our primary motivation in life is **to be connected with other people** - because it is the only **security** we ever have. Maintaining closeness is a bona fide **survival need**.

Through the consistent and reliable responsiveness of a close adult, infants, particularly in the six months of life, begin to trust that the world is a good place and come to believe they have some value in it.   The deep **sense of security** that develops fosters in the infant enough confidence to begin exploring the surrounding world, making excursions into it, and developing relationships with others - through racing back to mom, being held by her, and perhaps even clinging to her whenever feeling threatened.   In **secure attachment** lie the seeds for self-esteem, initiative, and even independence.   We explore the world from **a secure base**."

[Gibson, J.J. The Senses Considered as Perceptual Systems. p. 123]

"It is only half the truth to realize that animals feel the layout of the earth and its furniture. They also **seek contact with things** - at least some kinds of things and some kinds of contacts, for certain solids are beneficial and others are noxious. The infant clings to the mother and one adult clings to another in need. The earth itself has been compared to a mother in this respect. The metaphors of the **search for contact** hold true not only for the terrestrial, the sexual and the social realm, but also for the cognitive and the intellectual. One can be 'in touch' with other people, or with world affairs, or with reality."

[Gibson, J.J. The Senses Considered as Perceptual Systems. p. 132-133]

"The same can be said about each member of a sexual pair. Each partner is soft, warm, and suitably shaped to the other, and each touches when touched. **Social touch**, in fact, is a necessary basis of social life, and to be 'in touch' with one's fellows, or to **'make contact'** with other individuals, is a requirement for the development of a mental life. The perception of a concurrently soft, warm, round, and mobile thing is valuable to the young, and even to the old at certain times. They need it and seek it out, apparently, whether or not it yields satisfaction of hunger or sexual need. Matters are arranged so that it generally will, of course, **but the perception itself is satisfying**. We cling or clasp or embrace for its own sake."

[Kuspit, Donald B. The Subjective Aspect of Critical Evaluation. p. 80]

"Erich Fromm's conception of what he calls 'psychic needs' or 'existential needs' is one important formulation of these 'alternate,' more **psychologically primitive, needs**. To understand them in relationship to art is to gain an understanding of the kind of satisfaction art can afford and the kind of credibility a critical evaluation of art can have. Among the interpersonalists or proto-interpersonalists, Fromm's understanding of the **psychic needs** which arise from and articulate the 'conflict' which is ' man's essence,' and which 'enables and obliges him to find an answer to his dichotomies,' seems the most clearly and comprehensively formulated."

"It is because of this complicated tragic conflict that 'man 'is forced to overcome the horror of separateness, of powerlessness and of lostness, and find new forms of relating himself to the world to enable him **to feel at home**'.' The existential/psychic needs arise from this effort. Fromm identifies six of them: 'the need for relatedness, for transcendence, for rootedness, for a sense of identity, and for a frame of orientation and an object of devotion,' and 'for effectiveness.' Taken together, they dialectically articulate the unannulable tragic conflict at the core of life, without overcoming it."

[Kuspit, Donald B. The Subjective Aspect of Critical Evaluation. p. 81]

"**Instinctive relationship** to seemingly charismatic art prepares the way for transcendence of the old everyday self that superficially seems central. In general, I submit that the hierarchy of satisfactions is as follows, moving from the simplest or straightforward to the most complex **psychic need** art can seem to satisfy: (1) the need for effectiveness; (2) the need for relatedness; (3) the need for rootedness; (4) the need for transcendence; (5) the need for a frame of orientation and an object of devotion; and (6) the need for an experience of identity or unity."

[Kipnis, Jeffrey. Of Objectology. p. 102]

"Two factors collaborate in this forging (in both senses of the term) power of architecture. First are its physical quantities - how large it is, how much of it there is, how protractedly and repetitively **we are engaged with it**; I believe it was Lenin who remarked that quantity has a quality all of its own, a simple statement rooted in dialectical materialism, yet nevertheless, statement which, when one reflecting upon it closely, unfolds vast implications for architecture and for theories of the object in general. Secondly, are its quantities, the seminal interpretive relationships in terms of which we engage the architectural object including physical and **emotional shelter**, power, identity, status, beauty, and so forth. The significance of the quantity quality domain of architecture leads to the amplitude of the **transference** and **identification** which we form with that object, accounting, for example, for the 'maternality' of architectural space discussed by Bachelard. Hence architecture stands with family, state, and language as one of the principal formative arenas, yet its theorization has avoided the depth of scrutiny enjoyed by those other fields of study."

[Gehry, Frank. The Vitra Design Museum. p. 54]

"the volumes that seem to hover in midair tend also to render humanist conceptions of the body obsolete, or in any case, force the realization that the body itself is **a social construct**, not an absolute datum."

[Eisenman, Peter. The Affects of Singularity. p. 44]

"But if it can be said that if only by virtue of the relationship of media to reality that reality is no longer homogeneous but rather heterogeneous, then there are possibilities for conceptualising architecture. Within the mechanical paradigm the subject's relationship to the object was clearly understood since the mechanical paradigm evolved from the classical anthropocentric, organicist paradigm. There was a continuity; that is, with every change there was a homogeneity within each paradigm. The individual knew how to react to the object, even though the individual became clearly displaced from his or her centric position. It can be argued that architecture, even though it deals with the same physical individual with the same functional needs and the same **need for an affective response** to a physical space, no longer produces the same affect because of the shift of the human subject's relationship to the paradigm, that is, the shift from the mechanical to the electronic."

[Rapoport, Amos. History and Precedent in Environmental Design. p.303-304]
"Vernacular urban design is also the result of many decisions by many individuals and thus reflects shared schemata. The result is that such design expresses, in physical form, **what people need and want.** High-style spaces, on the other hand, often designed by individuals for individual patrons, may be highly idiosyncratic. They are also greatly influenced by design 'theories' most of which have little or no relationship to human behavior. They also tend to change much more frequently and abruptly than do vernacular designs (Rapoport, in press). Moreover, the choice process in terms of which design can be understood (Rapoport 1977) operates over long periods of time to arrive at forms. This means that they have been selected over long periods of time (Rapoport 1986c). Such forms, therefore, once again tend to reflect **consensual needs** and wants of large aggregates of people; they have become congruent with activities and are highly supportive of them (Rapoport, in press). If many such examples from many places and cultures, and over long periods of time, show the same, or similar, characteristics, one can be confident that these patterns are highly significant."

[Alexander, Christopher. A Pattern Language: Towns, Buildings, Construction. p. 930-931]
"Where can the need for concealment be expressed; the need to hide; the need for something precious to be lost, and then revealed? We believe that there is a **need** in people to live with a secret place in their homes: a place that is used in special ways, and revealed only at very special moments. To live in a home where there is such a place alters your experience. It invites you to put something precious there."
"An anthology devoted to small boxes, such as chests and caskets, would constitute an important chapter in psychology. These complex pieces that a craftsman creates are very evident witnesses of the need for secrecy, of an intuitive sense of hiding places. It is not merely a matter of keeping a possession well guarded. The lock doesn't exist that could resist absolute violence, and all locks are an invitation to thieves. A lock is a physical threshold."

[Ittelson, William H. and Proshansky, Harold M. An Introduction to Environmental Psychology: Research Methods in Environmental Psychology. p. 217]
"Gans concluded that the crowded setting was not in itself a major cause of pathology. The uprooting of

inhabitants (as part of an urban renewal project) was likely to be more contributory to mental illness. Because of strong family and ethnic ties- the area was largely Italian- any disruption of the social fabric was threatening to the inhabitants' **sense of security**. He found, too, that neighborhoods which urban planners perceive as a slum are not necessarily so perceived by those who live in them. A decrepit physical environment, in short, does not always mean a pathological social environment."

[Wilson, Colin St. John. The Natural Imagination: An Essay on the Experience of Architecture. p. 65]
"But our experience of architecture is far from being encompassed by such learned response and reflection. Indeed in the very first instance quite other responses are at work, a whole array of **instinctive reactions** triggered by the nervous system and marked above all by **the quality of immediacy**. One aspect of this instinctual reaction received its most celebrated formulation in aesthetic terms in the idea of Einfuhlung, or empathy, first defined by Robert Vischer and Theodor Lipps as the reincorporation of an **emotional state** or physical sensation **projected upon the object of attention**. Its popularised expression in architectural literature appears in Geoffrey Scott's 'Architecture of Humanism' where he writes: 'These masses are capable, like ourselves, of pressure and resistance...we have looked at the building and identified ourselves with its apparent state. We have transcribed ourselves into terms of architecture...It has stirred our physical memory...' Similarly Le Corbusier talks about the column as 'a witness of energy' and we are drawn into a world in which remote transpositions of the human figure participate in an exchange of forces, of pressure and release, of balance and counterbalance in which construct and spectator seem to become one. But in its confinement to aesthetic sensation alone, the notion of empathy is patently too limited: yet it does bear witness to a level of experience that has far deeper repercussions and that is as deeply rooted as it is paradoxically unacknowledged-the sense, however abstracted, of a body-figure and the ensuing notion of Presence that flows from it. Michelangelo (for whom the human body served as the supreme image for all that he had to say, both sacred and profane) in his one written statement about architecture testified to it when he wrote '...and surely architectural members derive from human members. Whoever has not been or is not a good master of the figure and likewise of anatomy cannot understand (anything) of it.' With this stress upon anatomy this statement far outruns the conventional concern with the abstractions of Vitruvian symmetry. This mode of experience is real, **active in us all**, compelling in its impact. I hope to trace the source of this body metaphor and, in so doing, to show that it goes beyond **instinctive sensation** and is structured like a language."

APPENDIX F: ALLURE

[Hogarth, William. The Analysis of Beauty. p.57]

"This way of composing **pleasing forms**, is to be accomplished by making choice of **variety of lines** , as to their shapes and dimensions; and then again by varying their situations with each other, by all the different ways that can be conceived: and at the same time (if a solid figure be the subject of the composition) the contents or space that is to be included within those lines, must be duly considered and varied too, as much as possible, with propriety. In a word, it may be said, the art of composing well is the art of varying well."

[Hogarth, William. The Analysis of Beauty. p.59]

"When you would compose an object of a great variety of parts, let several of those **parts be distinguished by themselves**, by their remarkable difference from the next adjoining, so as to make each of them, as it were, one well-shaped quantity or part, as is marked by the dotted lines in figure 35. T. p. 1, (these are like what they call passages in music, and in writing paragraphs) by which means, not only the whole, but even every part, will be better understood by the eye:"

"**Light and shade**, and **colours**, also must have their distinctness to make objects completely beautiful; but of these in their proper places - only I will give you a general idea of what is here meant by the beauty of distinctness of forms, lights, shades, and colours, by putting you in mind of the reverse effects in all of them together."

[Hogarth, William. The Analysis of Beauty. p.65-67]

"strictly speaking, there is but one precise line, properly to be called **the line of beauty**, which in the scale of them (Fig. 49 T. p.1) is number 4: the lines 5, 6, 7, by their bulging too much in their curvature becoming gross and clumsy; and, on the contrary, 3, 2, 1, as they straighten, becoming mean and poor;"

"It may be worth our notice however, that the stay, number 2, would better fit a well-shaped **man** than number 4; and that number 4 would better fit a well-formed **woman**, than number 2; and when on considering them, merely as to their forms, and comparing them together then, merely as to their forms, and comparing them together as your would do two vases, it has been shown by our principles, how much finer and more beautiful number 4 is, than number 2: does not this in our determination enhance the merit of these principles, as it proves at the same time how much the form of a woman's body surpasses in beauty that of a man? From the examples that have been given, enough may be gathered to carry on our observations from them to any other objects that may chance to come in our way, either animate or inanimate; so that we may not only lineally account for the ugliness of the toad, the hog, the bear and the spider, which are totally void of this waving-line, but also for the different degrees of beauty belonging to those objects that possess it."

"the knowledge of what I think the **sublime in form**, so remarkable displayed in the human body; in which, I believe, when he is once acquainted with the idea of them, he will find this species of lines to be principally concerned."

[Hogarth, William. The Analysis of Beauty. p.70-76]

"It will be sufficient, therefore, at present only to observe, first, that the whole horn acquires a beauty by its being thus genteely **bent two different ways**; secondly, that whatever **lines are drawn on its external surface** become graceful, as they must all of them, from the twist that is given the horn, partake in some degree or other, of the shape of the serpentine-line: and, lastly, when the horn is split, and the inner, as well as the outward surface of its shell-like form is exposed, the eye is peculiarly entertained and relieved in the pursuit of these serpentine-lines, as in their twisting their concavities and convexities are alternately offered to its view. Hollow forms, therefore, composed of such lines are extremely beautiful and pleasing to the eye; in many cases more so, than those of solid bodies. Almost all the muscles, and bones, of which the human form is composed, have more, or less of these kind of **twists** in them; and give in a less degree, the same kind of appearance to the parts which cover them, and are the immediate object of the eye: and for this reason it is that I have been so particular in describing these forms of the bent, and twisted and ornamented horn. There is scarce a straight bone in the whole body. Almost all of them are not only bent different ways, but have a kind of twist, which in some of them is very graceful; and the muscles annexed to them, though they are of various shapes, appropriated to their particular uses, generally have their component fibers running in these **serpentine-lines**, surrounding and conforming themselves to the **varied shape** of the bones they belong to: more especially in the limbs. Anatomists are so satisfied of this, that they take a pleasure in distinguishing their several beauties. I shall only instance in the thigh-bone, and those about the hips."

"such shell-like winding forms, mixed with foliage, twisting about them, are made use of in all ornaments; a kind of composition calculated merely to **please the eye**."

"the parts are too distinctly **traced by the eye**, for that intricate delicacy which is necessary to the utmost beauty;"

"but when these lines lose so much of their twists as to become almost straight, all elegance of taste vanishes."

"he will easily be led to see further, that this tendency to beauty is one, is not owing to any greater degree of exactness in the proportions of its parts, but merely to the more **pleasing turns**, and **intertwistings of the lines**, which compose its external form; for in all the three figures the same proportions have been observed, and, on that account, they have all an equal claim to beauty. And if he pursues this anatomical inquiry but a very little further, just to form a true idea of the elegant use that is made of the skin and fat beneath it, to conceal from the eye all that is hard and disagreeable, and at the same time to preserve to it whatever is necessary in the shapes of the parts beneath, to give grace and beauty to the whole limb: he will find himself insensibly led into the principles of that grace and beauty which is to be found in well-turned limbs, in fine, elegant, healthy life, or in those of the best antique statues; as well as into the reason why his eye has so often **unknowingly** been pleased and delighted with them. Thus, in all other parts of the body, as well as these, wherever, for the sake of the **necessary motion of the parts**, with proper strength and agility, the insertions of the muscles are too hard and sudden, their swellings too bold, or the hollows between them too deep, for their out-lines to be beautiful; na**ture most judiciously softens these hardnesses,** and plumps up these vacancies with a proper supply of fat, and covers the whole with the soft, smooth, springy, and, in delicate life, almost transparent skin, which, conforming itself to the external shape of all the parts beneath, expresses to the eye the idea of its contents with the utmost delicacy of beauty and grace. The **skin**, therefore, thus tenderly embracing, and gently conforming itself to the varied shapes of every one of the outward **muscles** of the body, softened underneath by the fat, where, otherwise, the same hard lines and furrows would appear,"

"to give a clear idea of the different **effect such anatomical figures have on the eye**, from what the same parts have, when covered by the fat and skin; by supposing a small wire (that has lost its spring and so will retain every shape it is twisted into) to be held fast to the out-side of the hip (figure 65, pl. 1) and thence brought down the other side of the thigh obliquely over the calf of the leg, down to the outward ankle (all the while pressed so close as to touch and conform itself to the shape of every muscle it passes over) and then to be taken off. If this wire be now examined it will be found that the general **uninterrupted flowing twist**, which the winding round the limbs would otherwise have given to it, is broke into little better than so many separate plain curves, by the sharp indentures it every where has received on being closely pressed in between the muscles. Suppose, in the next place, such a wire was in the same manner twisted round a living well-shaped leg and thigh, or those of a fine statue; when you take it off you will find no such sharps indentures, nor any of those regular engralings (as the heralds express it) which displeased the eye before. On the contrary, you will see how gradually the changes in its shape are produced; how imperceptibly the different curvatures run into each other, and how easily the eye glides along the varied wavings of its sweep."

[Hogarth, William. The Analysis of Beauty. p.79-80]
"We should therefore endeavor, in the next place, to vary them every way in our power, **without losing entirely the true idea of the parts themselves**. Suppose them then to have changed their situations a little, and slipped beside each other irregularly, (somehow as is represented in fig. 81. T. p. 2, merely with regard to their situation) and the external appearance of the whole piece of the body, now under our consideration, will assume the more varied and pleasing form, represented in fig. 76; **easily to be discerned by comparing the three figures** 76, 77, 78, one with another; and it will as easily be seen, that were lines to be drawn, or wires to be bent, over these muscles, from one to the other, and so on to the adjoining parts;"

"the application of this principle of **varying these lines, as their lengths will admit of**, will be found to have its effect as gracefully as in the more lengthened muscles of the body."

[Hogarth, William. The Analysis of Beauty. p.86-87]
"But in nature's machines, how wonderfully do we see **beauty and use** go hand in hand! Had a machine for this purpose been nature's work, the whole and every individual part might have had exquisite beauty of

form without danger of destroying the exquisiteness of its **motion**, even as if ornament had been the sole aim; its movements too might have been graceful, without one superfluous title added for either of these lovely purposes."

"Thus again you see, the more variety we pretend to give to our trifling movements, the more confused and unornamental the forms become; nay chance but seldom helps them. How much the reverse are nature's! The greater the variety her movements have, the more beautiful are the parts that cause them."

"It is also to be noted of every species, that the handsomest of each move best: birds of a clumsy make seldom fly well, nor do lumpy fish glide so well through the water as those of a neater make; and beasts of the most elegant form, always excel in **speed**; of this, the horse and greyhound are beautiful examples; and even among themselves, the most elegantly made seldom fail of being the swiftest."

[Hogarth, William. The Analysis of Beauty. p. 90-91]

"nay all the muscles shift their appearances in different movements, so that whatever may have been pretended by some authors, no exact mathematical measurements by lines, can be given for **the true proportion of a human body**."

"yet these sort of notions have so far prevailed by time, that the words, **harmony of parts**, seem as applicable to form, as to muscle."

[Hogarth, William. The Analysis of Beauty. p.95-97]

"Indeed, as many parts of the body are so constantly kept covered, the proportion of the whole cannot be equally known; but as stockings are so close and thin a covering, **every one judges** of the different shapes and proportions of legs with **great accuracy**. The ladies always speak skillfully of necks, hands and arms; and often will point out such particular beauties or defects in their make, as might easily escape the observation of a man of science. Surely, such determinations could not be made and pronounced with such critical truth, if the eye were not capable of measuring or judging of thickness' by lengths, with great preciseness. Nay more, in order to determine so nicely as they often do, it must also at the same time, trace with some skill those **delicate windings upon the surface** which have been described in pages 79 and 80, which altogether may be observed to include the two general ideas mentioned at the beginning of this chapter. If so, certainly it is in the power of a man of science, with as observing an eye, to go still further, and conceive, with a very little turn of thought, many other necessary circumstances concerning proportion, as of what size and in what manner the bones help to make up the bulk, and support the other parts; as well as what certain weights or dimensions of muscles are proper (according to the principle of the steelyard) to move such or such a length of arm with this or that degree of swiftness of force. But though much of this matter may be easily understood by common observation, assisted by science, still I fear it will be difficult to raise a very clear idea of what constitutes, or composes the **utmost beauty of proportion**."

"In doing which, we shall soon find that it is chiefly to be effected by means of the nice sensation we naturally have of what **certain quantities or dimensions of parts**, are fittest to produce the utmost **strength for moving, or supporting great weights**; and of what are most fit for the utmost **light agility**, as also for every degree, between these two extremes. He who hath best perfected his ideas of these matters by common observations, and by the assistance of arts relative thereto, will probably be most precisely just and clear in conceiving the application of the various parts and dimensions that will occur to him in the following descriptive manner of disposing of them, in order to form the idea of a fine-proportioned figure."

"when, as they approach each other in weight, their forms of course may be imagined to grow more and more alike, till at a certain point of time, they meet in just similitude; which being an exact medium between the two extremes, we may thence conclude it to be **the precise form of exact proportion**, fittest to perfect active strength or graceful movement;"

[Hogarth, William. The Analysis of Beauty. p.107]

"There is such a **subtle** variety in the nature of appearances, that probably we shall not be able to gain much ground by this inquiry, unless we exert and apply the full use of every sense, that will convey to us any information concerning them. So far as we have already gone, the sense of **feeling**, as well that of **seeing**, hath been applied to; so that perhaps a man born blind, may, by his better touch than is common to those who have their sight, together with the regular process that has been here given of lines, so see out the nature of forms, as to make a tolerable judgment of what is beautiful to sight."

[Hay, D. R. On the Science of those Proportions by which the Human Head and Countenance as Represented in Works of Ancient Greek Art are Distinguished from those of Ordinary Nature. p.31-33]

"The most remarkable characteristics in the structure of the human head are, its **globular form** (or rather such union of the globular and spheroidal forms as results, both in the external figure and in its sections, in the ovoid), and **the approximation of the plane of the face to a vertical line**; for in none of the lower animals does the skull present so near an approach to this form, nor the plane of the face to this direction."

"This species of **beauty** has been called the **ideal** in contradistinction to that of ordinary nature, from which it differs in being free from the deformities and peculiarities constituting the individuality by which men are distinguished from each other. Some writers upon beauty have asserted that there is no original, or positive beauty in the human countenance, and that our senses of the beautiful, as relative to it, arises from the association of ideas alone; while others affirm that this depends entirely upon expression. Sir Charles Bell, in his excellent essay upon the subject, has shown most clearly that such doctrines are erroneous, and that there exists in the permanent form of the human head and face an **innate beauty**, altogether **independent of the enhancement of expression, or of any association of ideas in the mind of the beholder**. He observes, that those who have hitherto written on the sources of beauty have not attained to the right principle, because they have not only lost sight of nature, but of what may justly be called the philosophy of the subject. In respect to the permanent form and beauty of the human head and face, in contradistinction to expression, Sir Charles says - 'Beauty of countenance may be defined in words, as well as demonstrated in art. A face may be beautiful in sleep, and a statue without expression may be highly beautiful.' 'But it will be said, there is expression in the sleeping figure, or in the statue. Is it not rather that we see in these the capacity for expression? - that our minds are active in imagining what may be the motions of those features when awake or animated? Thus, we speak of an expressive face before we have seen a movement, grave or cheerful, or any indication in the features of what prevails in the heart. Avoiding a mere distinction in words, let us consider, first, why a certain **proportion and form** of face is considered beautiful, and conveys the notion of capacity of expression; and, secondly, the **movements**, or the actual **expression of emotion**. I believe that it is the confusion between the capacity of expression and the actual indication of thought, that is the cause of the extraordinary difficulty in which the subject is involved.' "

[Hay, D. R. On the Science of those Proportions by which the Human Head and Countenance as Represented in Works of Ancient Greek Art are Distinguished from those of Ordinary Nature. p.37-39]
"The truth is, that we are more moved by the **features** than by the **form of the whole head**."
"We find its beauty and grandeur to depend more upon the degree of **harmony** amongst its parts, as to their **relative proportions and mode of arrangement**, than upon their excellence taken individually."

[Hay, D. R. On the Science of those Proportions by which the Human Head and Countenance as Represented in Works of Ancient Greek Art are Distinguished from those of Ordinary Nature. p.65-66]
"The distinction between the truly beautiful and the merely agreeable is clearly defined by Cousin. He observes - 'When we cast our eyes over existing nature, whether it be over the life that is called human, or that more extensive organic life, or even over inanimate nature, subject only to mechanical laws, we meet with objects that make us **feel pleasing or painful sensations. A form is present to your eyes**, and at the moment that you know it is, you feel an agreeable or a disagreeable sensation. If you are asked why it

pleases you, you cannot give a reason; if you are told that it displeases others, you are not surprised, because you know that sensibility is not constant, and that it is not necessary to dispute about sensations. Up to this point we have not slipped into the domain of art; **its object is beauty**, and we are but at the agreeable. Now, does it not sometimes happen that a form is not only agreeable to us, but, beyond this, that it appears beautiful to us? When we were asked why it was agreeable to us, we could only have answered, according to our individual right, 'I am the sole judge of what pleases or displeases me;' but when we are asked why we call this form beautiful, we appeal to an authority which is not our own, which is imposed on all men - the authority of reason.

'To the question, What are the characteristics of the agreeable and of the beautiful? we reply, that it will be shown presently that **unity, proportion, simplicity, regularity, grandeur,** and **generality**, appear more or less in objects that we call **beautiful**; and that **variety, motion, pliantness, energy,** and **individuality**, are marks of the **agreeable**.'

The want of a more extensive dissemination of such correct and comprehensive views upon this subject, has led to the erroneous notion that everyone has a right to hold his own opinions as to the beauty of proportion in works of formative art. The author, therefore, feels that he cannot recommend too strongly to his readers the study of Cousin's excellent work, from which the above extract is taken."

"The only pleasure of sense that our philosophers seem to consider, is that which accompanies **the simple ideas of sensation**; but there are vastly **greater pleasures in those complex ideas of objects**, which obtain the names of beautiful, regular, harmonious."

"It is of no consequence whether we call these ideas of beauty and harmony, perceptions of the external senses of seeing and hearing, or not. I should rather choose to call our power of perceiving these ideas an **internal sense**, were it only for the convenience of distinguishing them from other sensations of seeing and hearing which men may have without perception of beauty and harmony."

[Hay, D. R. Proportion, or the Geometric Principle of Beauty, Analyzed. p.1-2]

"Poetry is composed of two things, -of the natural perception of the beautiful, and of the artistic development of this perception. In the former sense we are all poets; in the latter sense only a few possess the divine gift, and merit the distinguished name. We are all poets; for we are all capable of seizing, among the aspects of the actual, **that harmony of proportions which constitutes beauty**, and of finding in the field of the possible and the spiritual, that image of perfection of which external grace and sublimity are simply the embodiments. The meanest event, the most insignificant object, if suggestive to us of brighter thoughts and deeper feeling than those that people the range of our ordinary musings, become for us a poetical event - **a poetical object**."

"**Proportion is**, in short, that geometrical quality in forms and figures by which they are rendered **pleasing** to the sense of sight, independently of their use or any other consideration."

[Hay, D. R. Proportion, or the Geometric Principle of Beauty, Analyzed. p.58]

"forms and figures as used in the arts require one or other of two qualities to render them pleasing: the first of which is the **imitation of natural objects**, and the second is **harmony**, produced by the proportion and arrangement of the elements of abstract form."

[Wollheim, Richard. The Image in Form: Selected Writings of Adrian Stokes. p. 38-39]

"And now I can explain fully what I mean by mass. **An effect of mass** is one connected with solidity or density of three-dimensional objects. **It is, therefore, in part an appeal to the sense of touch though the object be a building and not a piece of sculpture.** But solids afford an effect of mass only when they also allow the immediate the instantaneous synthesis that the eye alone of the senses can perform."

"Exploring sense of touch, I admit, introduces a succession, and therefore entails some element of **time** though it be turned into an instantaneous impression by the quickness of the perceiving eye."

"Mass reveals an entirety, reveals **space**, just as music dramatized succession or time with rhythm. And while admitting that when the eye perceives, other senses are always incited in that very act (for instance, I have inferred an oral appeal in Verona marble), and further, while admitting that visual art is bound to reflect responses of these other senses - for without them things perceived would not be objects - I consider that the basic appeal of the art of colour, painting, and of architecture, should be to the eye alone, just as music to the ear."

"Just as music can interpret any content in terms or rhythm, so painting can interpret any content in terms of **position**, of objects related by space."

[Kuspit, Donald B. Clement Greenberg: Art Critic. p.126]

"He recognizes that art always seems to fall back to its origins in life. The more we experience art the more charged with life it seems, and the less apparent the art in it is, i.e., the less aesthetic point it seems to have. Even the abstraction in abstract art comes to be devalued as such. It comes to seem simply a veil on a feeling for life, and indirect approach to it, **making it more alluring**. For Greenberg, modernism is a way of reminding us of the raw artistic datum left after the art in art has been debunked, as it were, by being reduced to its life reference. The modernist conception of art is what is left after spiritual understanding of it, which includes attention to art's psychological effect, has reminded us of its symbolic value and has in general viewed it as a device for 'raising consciousness.' But spiritual understanding of art altogether ignores the difficulty of materially making it, of creating that kind of quality which permits us in the first place to experience a work or art as powerful-and then to misread that power as a sign of life force, when in fact it is a sign of art force."

[Kuspit, Donald B. Clement Greenberg: Art Critic. p.144-145]
"Greenberg, then, claims to speak in the name of what Kant called 'a sensus communis, a sense or faculty that all human beings exercise similarly in esthetic experience.' Criticism is ideally an expression of the sensus communis; the critic is its spokesman. Kant 'failed to show...how this universal faculty could be invoked to settle disagreements of taste...judgment or appreciation.' Greenberg remedies this by arguing that consensus makes itself evident in judgments of aesthetic value that stand up under the ever-renewed testing of experience. Certain works are singled out in their time or later as excelling, and these works continue to excel: that is, they continue to compel those of us who in time after look, listen, or read hard enough. And there's no explaining this durability-the durability which creates a consensus-except by the fact that **taste is ultimately objective**."
"The best taste, like the best art, seems to transcend history-neither one really waits for history's judgment-because they are completely objective."

[Collins, John B. Perceptual Dimensions of Architectural Space Validated Against Behavioral Criteria. p. 4]
"animals raised in an **enriched visual and auditory environment** learn faster, grow better, and generally thrive, whereas animals raised in deprived environments with restricted stimuli, are smaller, learn slower, and are less able to cope with their environments. Support for the proposition has been gained in the observations that animals raised in enriched environments have larger, more massive portions of brain tissue than do other animals (Krech, 1962)."
"to assume that such findings can be generalized from animals to human beings is scientific nonsense, but to assume that they cannot be so generalized, is social suicide."
"enriching and enhancing the environment can do much to remedy the deprivation caused by poor social and poor learning environments. There has been much work recently in striving toward an increased understanding of environmental variables on learning rates, perceptual processes, cognitive growth, educational abilities: the general notion is that **an enriched enhanced environment enables the individual to better comprehend and deal with the world about him** (Deutsch, et al., 1968)."

[Collins, John B. Perceptual Dimensions of Architectural Space Validated Against Behavioral Criteria. p. 12]

"Attneave (see heath, 1968) has approached the problem of aesthetic factors from the standpoint of information theory and has suggested that some of the factors determining the **aesthetic merit** of a particular item include the economy of presentation of design as well as the equiprobability of any of its elements recurring."

"Garner (1962) has used a similar approach in the investigation of concept learning and concept formation. Following the same tradition Rump (1968) reports some preferences for **asymmetry, multiplicity and heterogeneity.**"

[Thiel, P. Notes on the Description, Scaling, Notation and Scoring of Some Perceptual and Cognitive Attributes of the Physical Environment. p. 594]

"the word envirotecture has been coined to fill the need for a general reference to a purposeful act of intervention in the physical environment (including the provision of new facilities and the management of existing facilities) which transcends these artificial boundaries and is concerned with continuous environmental experience. An envirotect then is a person engaged in environmental intervention on the basis of the continuous process of real-time experience, ultimately **to enrich the quality of this experience** and promote the development of individuals and groups experiencing this total environment. An envirotect does not design vehicles or rooms or buildings or gardens or cities; he designs **experiences** in any and all combinations of these parts of the environment."

APPENDIX G: INFLUENCE

[Endell, August. The Beauty of Form and Decorative Art. p.21]

"They teach us that there can be no new form, that all possibilities have been exhausted in the styles of the past, and that all art lies in an individually modified use of old forms. It even extends to selling the pitiful eclecticism of the last decades as the new style.

To those with understanding, this despondency is simply laughable. For they can clearly see, that we are not only at the beginning of a new stylistic phase, but at the same time at the threshold of a completely new Art. An Art with forms which signify nothing, and remind us of nothing, which arouse our souls as deeply and as strongly as music has always been able to do... This is the power of form upon the mind, **a direct immediate influence** without any intermediary stage... one of direct empathy."

[Wilson, Colin St. John. The Natural Imagination: An Essay on the Experience of Architecture. p.64]

"In the prologue to his celebrated panegyric on the Acropolis, Le Corbusier draws attention to a commonly felt distinction. 'You employ stone, wood and concrete and with these materials you build houses and palaces; that is Construction. Ingenuity is at work. But suddenly you touch my heart. You do me good, I am happy and I say: 'This is beautiful. That is Architecture'.' He then makes a series of references to 'a resonance, a sort of sounding-board which vibrates in ... an axis of organization'; and with Ozenfant (in the first number of L'Esprit Nouveau) he explores the 'physical-subjective facts which exist because the human organism is as it is'. But, to use Aalto's phrase, he did not go 'deep enough'. Some kind of revelation has occurred, in pure immediacy, unsought and unexplained: and that is a mystery. Most critics step down from the challenge because they do not have an explanation that is neat. But the mystery doesn't go away; **we can still be moved deeply by buildings** yet have no adequate terms to deal with the fact. We are normally very disinclined to talk about this in the same way that we find a verbal account of sexual attraction to be hopelessly inadequate. (There are some common features in the psychic chemistry of the two phenomena, a split-second immediacy of sensation, a mingling of the visual and the visceral, an uncanny awareness of some magnetic charge in the air, of a jolting presence, of time suspended.) For my own part I need to know why I can be so deeply moved in the presence of certain buildings."

"Clearly therefore the secret of this elation lies in the experience of some more primal conjunction of forms, as if to say that our experience of architecture is somehow divided in itself into frames of super- and infra-structure. **It is as if we are being manipulated by some subliminal code**, not to be translated into words, which acts directly on the nervous systems and the imagination at the same time, stirring intimations of meaning with vivid spatial experience as though they were one thing."

[Downs, R. M. and Stea, D. Image and Environment: Cognitive Mapping and Spatial Behavior. p.3]
"Psychoanalytic man, as delineated by Freud and Jung, was totally non-rational. His adult behavior was determined in large part by the (probably unconscious) resolution of psychological conflicts experienced earlier in life, and was influenced by biologically transmitted traces of earlier experiences in human evolution ('collective unconscious' or 'racial memory'). External factors were assumed to play a small role in adult patterns of decision-making: social influence was secondary, and environmental influence negligible.The only exception to this latter statement is the work of Searles (1960) who incorporated **influences from the physical (and spatial) environment into psychoanalytic thinking**."

[Downs, R. M. and Stea, D. Image and Environment: Cognitive Mapping and Spatial Behavior. p.5]
"Among theorists in psychology, Koffka (1935) may have been the first to distinguish **between the geographical environment (or absolute space) and the behavioral environment (or relative space),** although he acknowledges borrowing some concepts from Tolman. Koffka held that the geographical environment is not a stimulus or set of stimuli in itself, but is 'stimulus-providing', and that the mediation of

the behavioral environment clarifies the relationship between the geographical environment and behavior: Behavior takes place in a behavioral environment, **by which it is regulated**. The behavioral environment depends upon two sets of conditions, one inherent in the geographical environment, one in the organism. But it is also meaningful to say that behavior takes place in a geographical environment... (1) Since the behavioral environment depends upon the geographical, our proposition connects behavior with a remote instead of an immediate cause... (2) the results of the animal's behavior depends not only upon his behavioral but also on his geographical environment... The geographical environment, not only the behavioral, is changed through all behavior. (1935, p.31) Lewin, whose association with Tolman was closer, stressed the relationship of and distinctions among mathematical space, physical space, and psychological life space, concepts which resemble those of Koffka. Lewin developed a 'topological' or 'hodological' psychology, stressing the connection and paths between psychological regions: 'There is a certain topological structuring of the environment in nearly all situations with which psychology deals, and no doubt **there is always some structuring of the person**' (1936, p.62). For Lewin, the contrast between physical and psychological space stemmed from the laws appropriate to the two, with the determination of spatial relations in psychology dependent upon psychological processes and, hence, upon the nature and laws of psychological dynamics. While psychological life space was considered potentially 'metricisable' in the same sense that physical space is metric, Lewin also clarified distinctions between physical and psychological worlds via differing notions of connectedness and closure. The single connected space in which all physical reality is included does not exist within topological psychology, each life space being viewed as dynamically unique and equivalent to the totality of the physical world. The notion of 'dynamic closure' entered here as well, the physical world being considered as a 'dynamically closed' unity and the psychological world a dynamically enclosed unity."

[Maslow, A. H. and Mintz, N. L. Effects of Aesthetic Surroundings. p.466]
"It is concluded that **visual-esthetic surroundings** (as represented by the 'B' room and 'U' room) **can have significant effects upon persons exposed to them**. These effects are not limited either to 'laboratory' situations or to initial adjustments, but can be found under naturalistic circumstances of considerable duration."

[Hay, D. R. On the Science of those Proportions by which the Human Head and Countenance as Represented in Works of Ancient Greek Art are Distinguished from those of Ordinary Nature. p.5-6]
"In the science of Aesthetics, therefore, the human mind is the subjects, and external nature the object. Each individual mind may be considered as a monad in creation - a world within itself.   These two

separate existences - the individual mind and so much of creation as lies within the scope of its powers - have a distinct relation to each other: **the subject is affected by the object**, and the media of communication are the sensorium and its inlets, the organs of sense - the former being in direct contact with the subject, and the latter with the object. The organs of sense are thus acted upon in various ways, agreeably to the numerous modifications of the elements of the external world."

[Wollheim, Richard. The Image in Form: Selected Writings of Adrian Stokes. p.123-124]
"Formal arrangements can sometimes transmit a durable image. That is not merely to say that they are expressive. There is a sense in which every object of the outside world is expressive since we tend to endow natural things, any piece of the environment, **with our associations to it**, thereby constructing an identity additional to the one generally recognized. At heightened moments anything can gain the aura of a personage. But in art it should not be we who do all the imaginative work in this way. The better we understand art the less of the content we impose, **the more becomes communicated**. In adopting an aesthetic viewpoint - this, indeed, is a necessary contribution on our part - which we have learned from studying many works of art, we discover that to a considerable extent our attention is confined to **the relationship of formal attributes and of their image-creating relevance to the subject-matter**. The work of art should be to some extent a strait-jacket in regard to the eventual images that it is most likely to induce. Obviously any mode of feeling can be communicated by art, perhaps even by abstract art. Nevertheless the personification of this message in the terms of aesthetic form constructs a simulacrum, a presence that qualifies the image of the paramount feeling expressed. The feeling takes to itself as a crowning attribute more general images of experience. **Form, then, ultimately constructs an image or figure of which, in art, the expression of particular feeling avails itself.**"
"to construct from psychical and emotional as well as physical concatenations a thing that we tend to read as we read a face. A face records more experience than its attention at the moment we look at it. Perhaps all we demand of a work of art is that it should be as a face in this sense."

[Kuspit, Donald B. The Subjective Aspect of Critical Evaluation. p.82]
"The critical **relationship to art**, which I submit is the model relationship to it, begins interpersonally in the theatrical **mirror transference** - the work of art seems to promise a glimpse of one's deepest self, seems to reflect as through a glass darkly its basic unity of being."
"The art is encountered and analyzed in the aura of this two-facted narcissistic **transference**, out of which emerges a fantasy or transference representation of the artist-self, which is **internalized by the critic**. But it is in fact the critic's self 'making sense' of the art, that is, giving it a self of which the particular works are

regarded as emanations.   Through the process of unconsciously narcissistically oriented analysis of the art the critic simultaneously imagines and internalizes the artist-self, but in fact it is his own to begin with.   It may have constituted itself by imaginative **identification with the artist's work**, but its form pre-existed the work, not Platonically, but in the theatrical interpersonal space **of his relationship to it**, which arose and became consequential in the first place because of his expectation that art could satisfy his need for integral selfhood, indeed, was the royal road to it, the privileged path to an experience of identity or unity of self.   I think this expectation is socio-historically generated, but the key point here is that the critic becomes pregnant, as it were, with a sense of integrity, **through his relationship with art**."

[Kuspit, Donald B. Clement Greenberg: Art Critic. p.50-51]
"While unity is 'conclusive', its dialectical tension gives it 'crispness'.   This offsets unity's 'monumentality', which 'has little to do with size' but with the tightness of the coherence created by dialectical tension.   For Greenberg, the monumentality of unity has nothing to do with 'the logic of appearances' but with 'the logic of somatic structures'.   Unified form is a **somatic** structure for Greenberg, and he is acutely conscious of the tension which creates and sustains the structure, tightening it into coherence."

"Cramping is a step on the way to this surface vibrancy, which is finally achieved when pictorial space is sufficiently unified to 'erase the old distinction between object-in-front-of-background and background-behind-and-around-object, erase it at least as **something felt rather than merely read**'. Cubism first accomplished this: 'All space became one, neither 'positive' nor 'negative', **insofar as occupied space was no longer clearly differentiated from unoccupied**.   And the object was so much formed, as exhibited by precipitation in groups or clusters of facet planes out of an indeterminate background of similar planes, which latter could also be seen as vibrating echoes of the object.'   For Greenberg, the drama of interlocking positive and negative space, the determinate and indeterminate, into a tight yet still tense unity, repeatedly plays itself out in abstract art."

[Heider, Fritz. On Perception, Event Structure, and Psychological Environment. p.8]
"We have explained why some physical structures appear as objects of perception and some as mediators. The question now arises of how the perceptual significance of physical entities is related to their behavioral significance.   Not all parts of the environment are of equal significance for our action.   We do not have to know how the particles of the air move, but the fact that a chair stands here and a table there is important and can determine our behavior.   We have to be able to perceive a car that passes us in the street, the staircase of the house that we are entering.   We need to know only a few of the infinite number of possible determinations of the environment in order to be adequately oriented about the possible

relationships of our bodies to it. We live only in one particular level of this world; we have no relationship to many of the facts or events of our surroundings, they are not 'real' for us. In order to gain more understanding of the significance for behavior of the structures in the environment, we must start with a discussion of the solid units among which we live."

[Barker, Roger G. Ecological Psychology. p.1]
"These new methodological and conceptual problems arose in connection with a wide spectrum of psychological phenomena, for ecological psychology is concerned with other molecular and molar behavior, and with both the psychological environment (the life-space in Kurt Lewin's term; the world as a particular person perceives and is otherwise **affected by it**) and with the ecological environment (the objective, pre-perceptual context of behavior; the real-life settings within which people behave)."

[Barker, Roger G. Ecological Psychology. p.4]
"The view is not uncommon among psychologists that the environment of behavior is a relatively unstructured, passive, probabilistic arena of objects and events upon which man behaves in accordance with the programming he carries about within himself (Brunswik, 1955; Leeper, 1963; Lewin, 1951). But research at the Midwest Field Station and elsewhere indicates that when we look at the environment of behavior as a phenomenon worthy of investigation for itself, and not as an instrument for unraveling the behavior-relevant programming within persons, the situation is quite different. From this viewpoint the environment is seen to consist of highly structured, improbable arrangements of objects and events which **coerce behavior** in accordance with their own dynamic patterning. When, early in our work at the Field Station, we made long records of children's behavior in real-life settings in accordance with a traditional person-centered approach, we found that some attributes of behavior varied less across children within settings than across setting within the days of our children. We found, in short, that we **could predict some aspects of** children's **behavior** more adequately from knowledge of the behavior characteristics of the drugstores, arithmetic classes, and basketball games they inhabited than from knowledge of the behavior tendencies of particular children (Ashton, 1964; Barker & Gump, 1964; Raush et al., 1959,1960). It was the experience that led us to look at the real-life environment in which behavior occurs, with the methodological and theoretical consequences"

[Barker, Roger G. Ecological Psychology. p.9]
"The most primitive and simple thing we know about the ecological environment is that it has structure; it has parts with **stable relations between them**. One task is to describe this structure. It is clear that

structure cannot be discovered by observing a single part, such as the point of intersection of the environment with a particular person, or by considering the parts separately, one by one."

[Barker, Roger G. Ecological Psychology. p.10-11]

"**The Behavior** with which one is concerned must be identified. There are many levels of behavior, each of which has a special environmental context. In the present case we are interested in molar behavior, in the behavior of persons as undivided entities; we are not interested in the behavior of eyelids or glands. The problem of identifying and describing the ecological environment of behavior is an empirical one. It is necessary to observe and describe the environment in order to develop theories that later can guide further empirical investigation. The identification of the ecological environment is aided by the fact that, unlike the life-space, it has an objective reality 'out there'; it has temporal and physical attributes. Since the physical-temporal world is not homogeneous but exists in natural parts with definite boundaries, the ecological environment occurs in bounded units. Arbitrarily defined physical-temporal units will not, except by chance, comprise an environmental unit. Furthermore, the boundaries and characteristics of the ecological environment cannot be determined by observing the persons within it. The individual persons within a bounded unit of the ecological environment differ in psychological attributes; their **behavior** in the same environment will, therefore, differ. However, since people en masse can be expected to have common attributes, the inhabitants of identical ecological units will exhibit a characteristic overall extra-individual pattern of behavior; and the inhabitants of different ecological units will exhibit different overall extra-individual patterns of behavior."

[Barker, Roger G. Ecological Psychology. p.29-30]

"Physical forces. **Physical arrangements can enforce some patterns of behavior and prevent others**. School corridors, for example, allow locomotion in certain directions only, their narrowness prevents the playing of circle games, and the absence of chairs or ledges encourages standing and walking and discourages sitting or lying. The layout of streets and sidewalks, the size and arrangement of rooms, and the distribution of furniture and equipment are often important factors in coercing certain features of standing patterns of behavior and in restricting others. The physical forces impelling and hindering behavior do not have to be absolute, like a wall that cannot be breached; they can be effective by making actions of some kinds easier than others. It is physically easier to walk on the streets and sidewalks of Midwest than to cut across lots; even dogs follow the streets and sidewalks to a considerable degree. In these cases, **physical forces from the milieu mold behavior to conform to its shape**."

[Barker, Roger G. Ecological Psychology. p.34]

"The nomenclature of behavior settings presents difficulties. While a behavior setting is the total, extra-individual pattern of behavior and milieu, the common names of settings often refer to only one of these aspects. Although the name of the behavior setting Midwest Lake specifies its physical side, the pattern of the behaving persons and objects is an essential part of the setting. The physical lake, per se, without the behavior and objects is not a behavior setting."

[Stea, D. Space, Territory and Human Movement. p.13]

"But, as previously indicated, territorial manifestations exist on smaller levels too, on levels more readily amenable to empirical investigation. And it is my contention that these smaller territories are in some way **affected** or **shaped** by the designed environment; if the designed environment changes, the territory may also change."

[Stea, D. Space, Territory and Human Movement. p.16]

"In other words, with the alteration in the shape, size, boundedness and differentiation of the territorial cluster and of the territorial units came marked alteration in the behavior of the individual members."

[Ittelson, William H. and Proshansky, Harold M. An Introduction to Environmental Psychology: Research Methods in Environmental Psychology. p.229]

"It will be recalled that Barker with his colleagues Wright (1954) and Gump (1964) advanced the hypothesis that behavior is best studied in its everyday, 'natural' environment; they call this approach 'ecological psychology.' Obviously, however, one cannot observe all people in action at once. In fact, most of our activities occur in well-defined physical settings - a classroom, a bus, a playground, a park, a restaurant. Each of these environments becomes the context for a social setting that **imposes a specific type of behavior** (studying, riding, playing, relaxing, eating) on those who enter it. This is to say that the setting is defined by its social as well as its physical properties. Within the 'environment / behavior milieu' there is a 'stream of behavior,' and it is this stream that Barker and his associates measure through a detailed system of observation."

[Ittelson, William H. and Proshansky, Harold M. An Introduction to Environmental Psychology: Research Methods in Environmental Psychology. p.230]

"constitutes the identification of those **'discriminable phenomena external to any individual's behavior'** (1968, p.13) which have a bearing on it."

"Technically we can call these episodes sequential dependencies. Though thousands of such observations, Barker's staff has been able to describe the 'standing patterns of behavior' which make up the 220 'settings' of Midwest. Each has its own regulatory, even coercive (although by no means total), power to compel behavior to an appropriate pattern."

[Collins, John B. Perceptual Dimensions of Architectural Space Validated against Behavioral Criteria. p.1]
"The emergence of a psychology whose point of application is man's total environment can readily be demonstrated in the advent of a new literature, new professional societies, and centers of active research. The last several years have seen a growing bulk of articles, journals, and proposals dealing with man's interaction with the environment and **its effect on his behavior**."

[Collins, John B. Perceptual Dimensions of Architectural Space Validated against Behavioral Criteria. p.6-7]
"The effective investigation of the behavioral-environmental interface presupposes that interactions between perception and behavior must be quantifiable. In order to do this, the following propositions seem reasonable: 1. The quality of design is defined by its functional utility. 2. The quality of form is defined by the rate at which it discloses its function to the user. If these propositions be true, then an index of the goodness of form vis-a-vis function is given by the degree of correspondence or correlation between the perception or the form of the article and its utility or it function. Restated, the question reads: Can verbal self reports of behavioral criteria be predicted from verbalized perceptual dimensions? In design terms, the question is: Can the functional utility of a space be determined from the degree of form disclosure? Restated in design terms, the question becomes: Can behavioral criteria (functional utility) of the space be predicted from a number of perceptual dimensions (in verbalized form) which indicate its degree of disclosure of form?"

[Collins, John B. Perceptual Dimensions of Architectural Space Validated against Behavioral Criteria. p.84]
"Once these criteria have been articulated and elaborated, the designer must exercise his ingenuity in selecting those elements of visual and functional impact which should facilitate such behavior criteria. When the structure or design is completed, the designer must follow through and study those users of his environment to determine whether the specific visual and design considerations do in fact **impinge on the behaviors** of the users of his environment."

[Pearson, David. Making Sense of Architecture. p. 68]

" 'Far from being narrowly based upon any single sense of perception like vision, our **response** to a building derives from our body's total response to and perception of the environmental conditions which that building affords.' "

"As a sensory being, the human individual **responds** to many stimuli, both cosmic and terrestrial. We usually talk of possessing five primary senses - sight, touch, taste, hearing and smell. But **we are affected** by a far wider range of stimuli than we think. Rather than treating them as separate sensory stimuli, it is more accurate to perceive of them as all parts of an energy continuum."

"As we know, however (for instance from energies such as certain forms of radiation), just because we cannot sense such stimuli it does not mean that they are not **affecting us**. A well as the bodily senses, we also react to other kinds of sensory experiences of the mind and spirit; for example, **sense of place, space and form**, fitness and culture, and spiritual power."

"Today, most of us spend around 90 per cent of our time in cities, buildings and vehicles - environments definitely not conducive to health, sanity and well-being. On the contrary, the majority of urban built environments are poorly designed and managed, and constant exposure to them produces stress and illness - the symptoms of 'sick building syndrome' being part of a far wider malaise. Our senses have adapted to try and cope - and it is the coping that presents the trouble. In a world beset with increasing noise, unpleasant air, polluted water and vas smells, our senses become dulled, if not actually impaired or damaged. Visual information - advertising, television, magazines - has tended to make sight dominant over the other sensory inputs to ears and nose. Modern architecture, by and large, is a reflection of this limited palette of senses. In 1947 James Marston Fitch, Professor of Architecture at Columbia University, New York, detailed the shortcomings of modern buildings. He saw the architect as being predominantly 'form conscious,' failing to establish a holistic design synthesis using all the human senses. The main reason, he felt, was the overwhelming presence of technology. Its sheer ubiquity for the manipulation of the natural environment allowed the design professions to ignore nature and our sensory perceptions as basic factors. With a better understanding of the environment - thermal, atmospheric, luminous, sonic, anthropometric and biological - the designer could reach a 'higher level synthesis combining creative design and available technology better to meet modern building needs."

[Hay, D. R. Proportion, or the Geometric Principle of Beauty, Analyzed. p. 8-9]

"Although I have hitherto referred to the effects of forms upon one eye only, in order to be more explicit, these effects are much modified by the rays entering both our eyes simultaneously; hence the **mild and pleasing influence** of horizontal composition, and the **more powerful and grand impression** made by that which is vertical. These are the sensible effects of figure upon the organs of vision, and it is only of such that I mean to treat. My observations can therefore have no reference to any geometrical property in figures beyond what can be superficially depicted, as they are reflected upon the retina; for it is well known that we only find out by experience that bodies possess other dimensions than what may be thus appreciated. The effects of geometrical configuration on the eye are, in the first instance, regulated by the relation they bear to the conformation of that organ itself; hence the **soft influence** of those of the curved kind, and the acute and **more powerful** effect of those whose outlines are composed of angles. On the mode of proportioning these elements of form in the combinations of various figures, their effect upon the eye depends - when a proper mode is adopted, geometric beauty is the result, while the adoption of an improper mode results in deformity."

[Hay, D. R. Proportion, or the Geometric Principle of Beauty, Analyzed. p. 12-13]
"By the science of chromatics it has been shown that in colouring also there are three primary elements - blue, red, and yellow; and that the complete scale of the colourist has other four secondary or intermediate hues - purple, orange, green and neutral. The art of painting teaches the proper use of these, the harmony arising from which is in its simplest elementary kind merely sensual, although, like other harmonies, it can be made, in the hands of men of genius, and combined with subjects of an exalted kind, to produce powerful effects upon the mind through the sense by which it is appreciated. But there has, as yet been no systematic arrangement, or geometric principles of proportion, applied to form, by which harmony may with certainty be produced; although it has been universally acknowledged that there is a harmony and discord in the modes of combining forms, as certainly as harmony and discord can be produced by various modes of combining either sounds or colours."

[Hay, D. R. Proportion, or the Geometric Principle of Beauty, Analyzed. p. 16-18]
"The homogeneous simplicity of these figures consists, first, in the circle being the most perfect curve, and composed of one line drawn round one point, from which every portion is equidistant; secondly, in the equilateral triangle being composed of three sides, the smallest number possessed by any rectilinear figure, which sides are equal, and each of which, as well as each of its angles, are equidistant from one point; and thirdly, in the square being composed of four equal sides and four right angles, each side and each angles being also equidistant from one point, and the right angle itself being homogeneous. Without referring to the analogy of sound; it might be shown that from their configuration, compared to the conformation of the eye, the effects of those particular forms upon that organ entitle them to hold the situation amongst other forms in which I have placed them. The pupil of the eye is circular; hence the rays, or pencils of light,

which pass from external objects to the back of the inner chamber, or retina, are most easily transmitted when the object is circular, as already explained. The circle is, therefore, not only geometrically the most simple of the homogeneous forms, but naturally so in reference to the organ by which it is perceived. The square is the next most **constant form to the eye**, as its angles, although more in number, are less acute than those of the triangle, and are the exact mean between acuteness and obtusity. The triangle, of the three, is the figure which, from its being composed of acute angles and oblique lines, exercises **the most powerful influence** on that delicate organ. In this respect it corresponds to the note E in the diatonic scale in music; for compositions having that note for their key exercise the same relative influence on the ear. Indeed, round and acute are terms as often employed to express qualities of sound, as they are to express the particular configuration of objects presented to the visual organs. It is well known in chromatics, that the primary colour, blue, exercises **a softer influence** on the eye than either of the other two, red and yellow; and this no doubt occurs from its being the most allied to darkness or black of the three, and hence associating more intimately with the colour of the retina itself. The colour that stands next to it as a primary in the solar spectrum, is red, which consequently holds the situation that the triangle does in my series of forms; and this colour is well known to **affect the eye more forcibly** than the yellow, which, in the natural series, is furthest removed from the blue; so that the more acute effect of the triangle upon the eye, although holding a medial situation, is quite in accordance with the analogy of acoustics and chromatics."

[Hall, Edward T. Handbook for Proxemic Research. p. 8]
"Because it was noted that some of the JOBS trainees were **sensitive to the orientation of furniture** and tended apparently **unconsciously to line up objects,** it was decided to conduct a spatial orientation study of limited scope during the practice interview sessions. It attempted to record trainees' unconscious re-orientation toward or away from the interviewer. Position of the applicant's chair - sometimes in a normal position and occasionally in a different, even awkward position - was marked before the interview. Thus, we could determine precisely how much, if any, it had been moved during the session. Photographic records were made of the positioning of chairs. This set of observations represents a sort of footnote to the main study, but it was revealing in that it confirmed an aspect of black behavior that had been previously observed, i.e., that the blacks with whom we were working were when compared to most whites extraordinarily **sensitive** to spatial arrangement. When an interviewee would enter the room it was observed that as he seated himself he would unconsciously align his chair with some other feature of the room, usually the side of the desk. Experimentally moving the chair out of line as little as 1/10th of an inch produced almost imperceptible precise realignment with the original object. Thus we found that the

research setting itself can be the subject of research."

[Winkel, G. H. and Sasanoff, R.   An Approach to an Objective Analysis of Behavior in Architectural Space. p. 360]

"The results of the factor analysis were studied to see if they would provide information on **the relationships** between particular paths taken and sets of exhibits which were visited by the sample. It was possible to subdivide the paths taken from each of the adjunctive galleries (maritime, animal, and ramp area) as well as the main entrance, and relate the direction taken from each of these points (either right, straight, or left) with the set of exhibits seen by each visitor. Such information provided **a more quantitative estimate of the behavior** of our visitors to the museum."

[Alp, Ahmet Vefik.   An Experimental Study of Aesthetic Response to Geometric Configurations of Architectural Space. p. 149]

"Population growth and advances in technology are two characteristic phenomena of our epoch. One of their primary consequences has been the increased density of populations in urban areas, which, in turn, has been one of the major causes of a gradual loss in the aesthetic quality of the built environment. The transition from beautiful to ugly, with the possible exception of a few elite places in some wealthier and culturally established regions of the world, has also been mentioned by many critics of art and architecture who on various occasions, have expressed the gradual extinction of **aesthetic sensitivity** and the need for greater perceptual richness in today's visual environment."

"aesthetic behavior characterizes virtually every level of human activity so constantly and closely that we are unconscious of its existence (2). A. H. Maslow identifies aesthetic satisfaction as a higher-level human need (3) and calls for the architectural profession to meet people's visual needs while providing them with aesthetic pleasure.   In order to succeed at this, architects and environmental designers first need to determine people's **affective responses** to a variety of buildings and building complexes. This research attempts a contribution in this domain: Geometry as a physical variable of the architectural space is manipulated under experimental conditions and the corresponding aesthetic reactions are systematically evaluated."

"The geometry of the architectural space was the independent variable and its possible aesthetic- emotional effects constituted the dependent variable for the study."

[Eisenman, Peter. The Affects of Singularity. p. 43]

"There are two English words, 'affect' and 'effect', that sound alike but mean quite different things. Effect is something produced by an agent or cause. In architecture it is the relationship between some object and its function or meaning; it is an idea that has dominated Western architecture for the last 200 years. Since the French Revolution, architecture, in its political, social and economical sense, has dealt with effect. If it is good it is effective: if it is good it serves more people. The clearest example of effect is the utilitarian creed of modern architecture; form follows function. This argued that a socially viable programme, properly elaborated, would provide good architecture. Affect, on the other hand, has nothing necessarily to do with good. Affect is the conscious subjective aspect of an emotion considered apart from bodily changes. Affect in architecture is simply **the sensate response to a physical environment**."

[Alexander, Christopher. A Pattern Language: Towns, Bulidings, Construction. p.884]
"But these biological rooms are as irrational, as much based on images and fantasies as the rigid crystals they are trying to replace. When we think about the **human forces acting on rooms**, we see that they need a shape which lies between the two. There are reasons why their sides should be more or less straight; and there are reasons why their angles, or many of them anyway, should be rough right angles. Yet their sides have no good reason to be perfectly equal, their angles have no good reason to be perfectly right angles. They only need to be irregular, rough, imperfect rectangles. The core of our argument is this. We postulate that every space, which is recognizable and walled enough to be distinct, must have walls which are roughly straight, except when the walls are thick enough to be concave in both directions. The reason is simple. Every wall has **social spaces** on both sides of it. Since a social space is convex - see the extensive argument in positive outdoor space (106) - it must either have a wall which is concave (thus forming a convex space) or a wall which is perfectly straight. But any 'thin' wall which is concave toward one side, will be convex toward the other and will, therefore, leave a concave space on at least one side."

APPENDIX H: REFINEMENT

[Skalski, Martin. Theory of Design Mutation. p.102]

"But, it shouldn't be just the forms in nature that interest the designer, but how the actual forms develop." "I think that **internal emotions and sensibilities of living beings can be a cause of natural mutation** in natural forms, and that we, as humans, can also find new and relevant design concepts through the pure use of our emotions and sensibilities."

[Alexander, Christopher. A Pattern Language: Towns, Buildings, Construction. p.926]

"Before you build the seat, get hold of an old arm chair or a sofa, and put it into the position where you intend to build a seat.   Move it until you really like it.   Leave it there for a few days.   See if you enjoy siting in it.   Move it if you don't.   When you have got it into a position which you like, and where you often find yourself sitting, you know it is a good position.   Now build a seat that is just as wide, and as well padded - and your built-in seat will work."

[Hogarth, William. The Analysis of Beauty. p.62]

"Have not many gothic buildings a great deal of consistent beauty in them?   Perhaps acquired by a series of **improvements made from time to time** by the natural persuasion of the eye,"

[Hogarth, William. The Analysis of Beauty. p.93-94]

"There is a **medium** between these, proper for every character, which the eye will easily and accurately determine."

"no rule or compasses would decide this matter either so quickly or so precisely as **a good eye**. It may be observed, that minute differences in great lengths, are of little or no consequence as to proportion, because they are not to be discerned; for a man is half an inch shorter when he goes to bed at night, than when he rises in the morning, without the possibility of its being perceived."

"Thus much I apprehend is sufficient for the consideration of general lengths to breadths.   Where, by the way, I apprehend I have plainly shown, that there is no practicable rule, by lines, for minutely setting out proportions for the human body, and if there were, the eye alone must determine us in our choice of what is most pleasing to itself.

Thus having dispatched general dimension, which we may say is almost as much of proportion, as is to be seen when we have our cloaths on: I shall in the second and more extensive method proposed for considering it, set out in the familiar path of common observation, and appeal as I go on to our usual feeling, or joint-sensation, of figure and motion."

[Maslow, A. H. and Mintz, N. L. Effects of Aesthetic Surroundings. p.460]

"Recognizing the situational nature of our definitions of 'beauty', 'average' and 'ugly', there still are interesting implications if our research would continue to find the effects of 'average' surroundings to lie closer to those of 'ugly' than those of 'beauty', rather than finding that effects of 'average' lie midway between the two, or closer to 'beauty'.   This, of course, would have immediate relevance for professors and their offices."

[Hay, D. R. Proportion, or the Geometric Principle of Beauty, Analyzed. p.10]

"The smallest number of parts by which this element is attainable are **two**, and the greatest number **three**."

APPENDIX I: BEHAVIOR

[Canter, David. Psychology for Architects. p.152-153]

"One way of summarising the contribution of psychology to architecture is by suggesting that, somewhat paradoxically, it is the view of man which psychology provides which is its greatest contribution. This is the view, in lay terms, of what 'makes people tick'. Or slightly more technically, the appropriate 'model of man'. If a designer sees people as essentially **passive**, responding to the pressures of his building in a simple and direct way, then this will shape the building form which he produces. On the other hand a model which has its roots more directly in organic or biological analogies, which sees people as consciously trying to **adapt to**, and   sense of, their environment leads to a different (and often more indeterminate) type of architecture. The great dangers of the 'self-fulfilling' prophecy require that these models are brought out into the open and tested objectively. For instance, a building which limits the possibilities of adaptation will tend to encourage regular, unvaried **behaviour**. If the designer looks at this behaviour he will say; 'There I told you. People don't need adaptable buildings'. Thus a mechanical model of man on the part of the designer may lead to mechanical-like behaviour on the part of the users. Here perhaps lies the strength of the academic psychologist's approach over the architectural practitioner. Where the architect can only really test the degree to which the **patterns of behaviour**, in the buildings he designs, fit his implicit or explicit views of how and why people behave, the academic, working with his abstract stimuli and often more or less independently of real world problems, can test and compare the basic models he has of how and why people behave as they do. His conclusions on this are the essence of what he has to pass on to those who must apply his findings."

[Wheeler, L. Behavioral Slide Rule for College Architects. p.106]
"Behavioral science - the analysis of man's interaction with his environment - is a new tool for designers and architects."
"and the development of a new creative kinship between the architect and the social scientist, the communications expert, and the anthropologist."

[Stea, D. Space, Territory and Human Movements. p.13]
"We tend to regard space, in the designed environment, as defined by physical barriers which are erected to restrict motion and the reception of visual and auditory stimuli. In fact, it is also defined by the behavior of organisms occupying the space. The characteristics of their **spatial behavior** are many, but several similar ones have been grouped under the general heading 'territoriality'.
"In civilized man, aggression is highly socialized, so we cannot always use this form of overt behavioral expression as an index. Nevertheless, we have reason to believe that **'territorial behavior,'** the desire both to **possess** and **occupy** portions of space, is as pervasive among men as among their animal forebears - witness the attitude of slum-area street gangs toward their 'turf.' There is some suggestion, coming largely from the animal world, that territorial possession, as had originally been supposed, but is equally or even more fundamental."

[Stea, D. Space, Territory and Human Movements. p. 16]
"This relates to what some architects may mean when they speak of space and sense of space, to the problem of the familiar path in the Umwelt (phenomenal world) described by Jakob von Uexkull three decades ago. Thirty years later, John Barlow suggested that von Uexkull's three sensory spatial cues could be reduced to two: sense of direction and sense of distance. From recent experiments with human and animal subjects, we know that humans are not the only ones who tend to alter their **familiar paths** in retracting a point-to-point route. But we do not really know very much about the variables controlling the

establishing of familiar paths in designed environments. That no two human Unwelten are the same implies that even two **objectively** identical familiar paths are **subjectively** different. The difficulty one experiences in finding one's way about a city on the basis of directions given by a friend."

[Rapoport, Amos. History and Precedent in Environmental Design. p.246-247]

"it is likely that even if people are 'unaware' of their **needs**, they will respond to characteristics of settings appropriate to walking, select such settings for walking, and walk more in settings possessing these. This congruence between walking and supportive characteristics should be most in evidence in settings specifically created for walking, when that was the only, or principal travel mode."

"the effect of environments on people. That hinges on the validity of the notion of **environmental determinism.** The evidence makes it quite clear that the design of the physical environment alone cannot lead people to engage in any activity. Moreover, it is easier to be negatively determining, that is, to block given behaviors by making them impossible or very difficult, than it is to be positively determining - to generate activities or behaviors. In other words, motivation may overcome unsuitable environments, at a cost, but environments cannot generate motivation (Rapoport 1968a, 1969c, 1977, 1983c). Given the motivation or predisposition to walk, for example, the question becomes, What physical characteristics of the environment are most congruent with, and supportive of, such behavior?"

"People are not, in general, put into environments that then **affect them**. Rather they select environments, leaving those they find undesirable and seeking out desirable ones; there is a choice of settings based on preference (Rapoport 1977, 1980b, 1983c). This notion of **habitat selection** is very basic and, although derived from ecology, seems to apply very well to humans (e.g. Rapoport 1985b). One can study how different individuals and groups make different choices using different priorities and consequently are distributed differentially across different settings; not all settings attract people equally. This choice process involves an interplay on inborn characteristics and experience."

"it then becomes necessary to distinguish between **wants** and **needs**, but this needs to be done very cautiously and on the basis of reliable knowledge (Rapoport, 1980b, 1985b). The question being considered is which kinds of habitats, that is, settings will be (or would be) selected for pedestrian activities. Note, however, that pedestrian activities consist of two major kinds: **dynamic**, for example, walking and strolling; and **static**, for example, sitting or resting (e.g. DiVette 1977; Rapoport 1977, pp. 246-247). Both are pedestrian in the sense that people are not riding or driving; in that sense both are likely to differ from settings for traffic. Given that there are many possible types of space (Rapoport 1970b, 1977), both the preceding examples are pedestrian in contradistinction to traffic/motorist spaces, that is, **human space** rather than machine space."

"Dynamic and static spaces are likely to have, or require, different characteristics. **Movement spaces** tend to be linear, narrow, and have high complexity levels so that they entice with hidden views, encouraging walking, strolling, and sauntering. **Rest spaces** tend to be more static and wider, frequently contain greenery, require sitting facilities, and so on. Such spaces, whether plazas or avenues, encourage visual exploration from one spot - mainly of other people; they need to act as stages for social behavior for people who become objects of interest and provide the requisite complexity levels."

"There is also evidence that different perceptual processes operate in linear spaces (streets) and nonlinear spaces."

[Rapoport, Amos. History and Precedent in Environmental Design. p.253]

"I am concerned with perceptual variables as opposed not only to cultural but also as opposed to **cognitive** (having to do with orientation, imageability, and the like) (e.g. Lynch, 1960; Rapoport 1977); and also opposed to **associational**. This means that very little explicit consideration is given to the meaning of such settings. In practice, of course, these two aspects cannot easily be disentangled. It is likely that settings with perceptual characteristics supportive of pedestrian movement are also settings that signify or communicate their appropriateness for such behavior and activities."

"Yet **meaning** is important because, as already indicated, one is dealing not only with manifest and instrumental functions but also with latent aspects, among which meaning plays the most important role. In choosing such settings, certain perceived characteristics are matched against certain expectations, norms, images, and so on, which makes this process conceptually similar to other forms of habitat selection based on perceived environmental characteristics (Rapoport 1977, especially chapter 2; 1980b). It can, however, also be argued that meaning is more important in the case of pedestrian **static** settings (such as plazas) than of settings for pedestrian **dynamic** behavior, such as streets."

[Barker, Roger G. The Stream of Behavior. p.1-3]

"**Temporal aspects of behavior** are among the most compelling in experience and among the most easily measured of all of behavior's unnumbered characteristics. Despite the saliency of the time dimension however, little is known about the actual arrangement of behavior along its temporal axis. The studies reported in this volume attempt to push forward on this frontier; they are all empirical approaches to the stream of behavior and they have had to cope with some common problems."

"The stream of behavior can be divided into an infinite number of parts. These countless parts of the behavior continuum are of two types so far as their origin along the time dimension is concerned. One type, here called **behavior units**, consists of the inherent segments of the stream of behavior. The boundaries of behavior units occur at those points of the behavior stream where changes occur independently of the operations of the investigator. Alpha waves, psychotic episodes, and games of marbles are behavior units. Behavior units enter psychology when investigators function as transducers, observing and recording behavior with techniques that do not influence its course."

"The other parts of the behavior stream may be appropriately called **behavior tesserae**. Tesserae are the pieces of glass or marble used in mosaic work; they are created or selected by the mosaic maker to fulfill his artistic aims. Similarly, behavior tesserae are fragments of behavior that are created or selected by the investigator in accordance with his scientific aims."

"**Behavior Units** are **natural** units in the sense that they occur without intervention by the investigator; they are self-generated parts of the stream of behavior. **Behavior tesserae**, on the other hand, are alien parts of the behavior stream in the sense that they are formed when an investigator, ignoring or dismantling the existing stream of behavior, **imposes** or chooses parts of it according to his own preconceptions and intentions."

"The identification and description of the natural entities or events of a science, and of their relevant contexts or environments, and the incorporation of these into a unified system of concepts constitutes the **ecological** side of science."

"Even in the case of so precisely contrived a system as geometry, and such a static, natural system as the earth's surface, an interaction is evident in the superimposed maps of eastern Kansas."

"In this task they were tough-minded like the surveyors; they allowed few natural features of the behavioral terrain to interfere with the structures imposed by their experiments, tests, questionnaires, and interviews. They imposed a geometry upon behavior, **a geometry** grounded upon the axioms of experimental design and statistical methods, a geometry which reveals nothing directly about the **behavioral surface** upon which it is imposed."

[Barker, Roger G. The Stream of Behavior. p.20-21]

"The empirical study of behavior units and their temporal arrangement is a central issue in history, in linguistics, in music, in the literary arts, and in the dance. Laymen, too, find the **structure of the behavior stream** to be a manageable phenomenon, and they have much practical knowledge of it. In the ordinary course of like, the beginning and the end of actions are of utmost importance, for awareness of the arrangement of a person's own and his associates' behavior streams is the basis of effective social behavior."

"the stream of behavior is not a formidable datum, that it occurs in bursts, pauses, and pieces of many sorts which can be described and evaluated for both scientific and practical purposes."

[Barker, Roger G. The Stream of Behavior. p.23]

"Is the **stream of behavior** seen as a **continuum** or as a **sequence** of discrete units? If the latter, do different people see the same units? People behave toward others, and they speak and write about their own and other's behavior as if they perceive behavior in units; and the degree of harmony with which interacting individuals guide their behavior suggests considerable agreement regarding the beginning and end-points of the behavior units they discern."

[Barker, Roger G. Ecological Psychology. p. 11]

"Such **physical-behavioral units** are common phenomenal entities, and they are natural units in no way imposed by an investigator. To laymen they are as objective as rivers and forests, and they can be defined by denotation; they involve, in the beginning, no theories or concepts; they are parts of the objective environment that are experienced directly as rain and sandy beaches are experienced. An initial practical problem of ecological research is to identify the **natural units** of the phenomenon studied. The essential nature of the units with which ecology deals is the same whether they are physical, social, biological, or behavioral units: (a) they occur without feedback from the investigator, they are self- generated; (b) each unit has a time-space locus; (c) an unbroken boundary separates an internal pattern from a differing external pattern."

[Barker, Roger G. Ecological Psychology. p. 16-17]

"with some effort and experience the extra-individual assemblies of behavior episodes, behavior objects, and space that surround persons can be observed and described."

"Such entities stand out with great clarity; they are common phenomena of everyday life. We have called them K-21 behavior settings (frequently shortened to **behavior settings** and settings in the text). Studies of K-21 behavior settings provide evidence that they are stable, extra-individual units with great coercive power over the behavior that occurs within them."

[Barker, Roger G. Ecological Psychology. p. 19-20]

"The **behavior-milieu parts** are called synomorphs. The physical sciences have avoided phenomena with behavior as a component, and the behavioral sciences have avoided phenomena with physical things and conditions as essential elements. So we have sciences of behavior-free objects and events (ponds, glaciers, and lightning flashes), and we have sciences of phenomena without geophysical loci and attributes (organizations, social classes, roles). We lack a science of things and occurrences that have both physical and behavioral attributes. Behavioral settings are such phenomena; they consist of behavior-and-circumjacent-synomorphic-milieu entities. We call these parts of behavior setting behavior-milieu synomorphs, or more briefly, synomorphs. Structurally a behavior setting is a set of such synomorphs."

[Barker, Roger G. Ecological Psychology. p. 26-27]
"In addition to their essential, unvarying, structural and dynamic attributes, behavior settings have many other properties. Those we have studied will now be briefly described;"

"**Geographical locus**. Every behavior setting has a precise position in space which can be designated with the degree of precision the investigation requires."

"**Temporal locus, serial occurrence, and duration**. Behavior settings may occur only once, on a specified day, or they may recur according to some temporal schedule of days."

"**Population**. A behavior setting has a definite number of inhabitants at each occurrence. This population can be identified with respect to whatever attributes are relevant, such as age, sex, social class, town residents, nonresident inhabitants."

"**Occupancy time**. The number of person-hours a behavior setting is occupied over a designated period of time is the occupancy time of the setting for that period; it is the product of the mean population per occurrence and the duration in hours of all occurrences."

"**Functional position of inhabitants**. Behavior settings have an internal structure, and individuals and categories of individuals occupy the various parts to different degrees. An important feature of the internal structure of a behavior setting is the power that different parts exercise over its functioning."

"We have called this dimension of the internal structure of behavior settings the penetration dimension; and we have called those parts of setting with some direct power over all or a part of its functioning the performance zones; persons who inhabit performance zones are performers."

"**Action patterns**. The pattern of behavior of a setting has limitless attributes."

"**Behavior mechanisms**. The behavior pattern of a setting involves different effector systems to various degrees. The degree of involvement of the following mechanisms has been systematically studied; affective, gross motor, manipulation, verbal and thinking mechanisms."

"**Pressure**. Behavior settings differ in the degree to which they bring pressure upon different population subgroups to enter and participate in them."

[Craik, K. H. The Comprehension of the Everyday Physical Environment. p.33]
"**Motational systems** have been developed as standardized methods, akin to choreographic notation systems, whereby trained observers may note the sequence of principal elements and features in the

experience of moving through environmental displays, as in the movement along highways and pedestrian pathways."

[Eisenman, Peter. The Affects of Singularity. p.45]

"But crucial to this argument, is the fact that the mediated behaviour of today does not come from any **personal or individual form of behaviour**; it is collective behaviour. Media not only sets out to destroy the possibility of individual affect in order to be affective itself, but also must substitute **effect** for **affect**. Media assumes that an affective message must be an effective one and this influence alone has entirely altered our concept of affect as well as **individual behaviour**. For example, media cannot tolerate the possibility of mistake, the misgotten message, error and untruth, all of which are part of the possibility of affect.

Architecture not only does not deal with affect but it no longer deals with effect as well as strong media. Then how does architecture stand in the face of media, and specifically with the loss of the affecting aspect of individual expression. A possible way of returning architecture to the realm of affect may not be through the idea of the individual or the expressive, or through any kind of standardization or repetition of a norm but, in fact, through an idea of singularity.

Architecture - now operating as weak media - needs to regain the possibility of an affective discourse. The term singularity begins to explore the possibility of a discourse which brings to the electronic paradigm what particularity, individuality, personal expression was to the mechanical paradigm. That is a general context for exploring the possibility of an architecture of affect. It begins to suggest a contemporary notion of how architecture which is seen as singular can operate as weak media in an affective way within the electronic paradigm.

One way to approach the question of affect in architecture is by looking at the difference between singularity and individual expression, and to answer the questions: 'Why is individual expression no longer valid?' and 'Why is singularity not merely a form of expressionism?' The difference is at the heart of the idea of singularity.

Singularity, as the Japanese critic, Kojin Karatani, suggests is the difference between 'I' the **individual subject** and the 'I' which belongs to the general category of **everybody**."

APPENDIX J: PATTERN

[Alexander, Christopher. A Pattern Language: Towns, Buildings, Construction. p.x]

"The elements of this language are entities called **patterns**. Each **pattern** describes a problem which occurs over and over again in our environment, and then describes the core of the solution to that problem, in such a way that you can use this solution a million times over, without ever doing it the same way twice."

[Rapoport, Amos. History and Precedent in Environmental Design. p.214-215]

"Note that the last five or six sections can all be seen as having one major goal: to aid in the identification of regularities, that is, in the search for **pattern**. This is, of course, a major topic in recent discussions about science and, as the debate about making archaeology into a science has developed, so has an emphasis on the importance of pattern recognition. Recall my argument that a major consequence of such a search and a precondition for it is the use of the broadest and most diverse bodies of evidence and comparative analysis.

Thus in dealing with the issue of faunal remains, the point is made about the importance of recognizing distinctive (**"diagnostic"**) **patterns**. Only from those can one recognize or identify the agents responsible (Binford 1981). Although the specific emphasis in the latter is on bones, the argument about the importance of pattern recognition is, as pointed out above, very general. For "bones," one could substitute other "things"; the specific indicators, measures, methods, and inferential arguments would be different, but the importance of pattern recognition is general would remain because from **patterns** one can derive the expected composition (in this case, bone assemblages) and compare these with the actual ones. As discussed in Chapter 3, anomalies can only be identified if there are expectations. Having identified patterns and having concluded that they are interesting, one can then ask what they mean and make inferences about what happened in the past to result in such patterns. Ideally, of course, alternative explanations should be sought.

This theme of looking for **patterns**, one of the most basic activities of all scientists (and scholars), is a common theme in the recent literature in archaeology. This may be called repeated patterns of coocurrence (Smith 1982), or regularities (Salmon 1982). They may bear different labels (Binford 1981, 1983a,b; Renfrew 1982, 1984; Renfrew, Rowlands, and Segreaves 1982; Smith 1977), but the essence is the same: the importance of identifying **patterns** the material record, in the relationships among attributes, in behavior and in environment-behavior interaction for the purpose of using such regularities as analogs for inference."

[Rapoport, Amos. History and Precedent in Environmental Design. p.297]
"The case study approaches its subject matter from two sides, an approach of great importance in research generally. On the one hand, it begins with pedestrian behavior and its relation to complexity."
"On the other hand, it begins with the observation that most past vernacular environments seem to have a particular form. In that sense, it begins with what seems to be a **pattern**. It also seems, on the basis of personal intuitive feelings, anecdotal evidence, and the writing of certain design writers that this form of vernacular streets is highly supportive for pedestrians."

[Heider, Fritz. On Perception, Event Structure, and Psychological Environment. p. 79]
"Only nonlocal proximal determinants are accepted, and that means for Gestalt theory that external determination is made in terms of **stimulus patterns**, internal determination in terms of fields and Gestalt processes. Koffka (1935) states: All we intend to do is to replace laws of local correspondence, laws of machine effects, by laws of a much more comprehensive correspondence between the total perceptual field and the total stimulation...(p. 97). Things look as they do because of the field organization to which the

proximal stimulus distribution gives rise (p. 98). Thus we find the program of Gestalt psychology to be: perceptual processes have to be defined in terms of **stimulus pattern** and field organizations; the question, 'Why do things look as they do?' should be answered in these terms."

[Barker, Roger G. Ecological Psychology. p.18]
"A behavior setting has both structural and dynamic attributes. On the structure side, a behavior setting consists of one or more standing patterns of behavior-and milieu, with the milieu circumjacent and synomorphic to the behavior. On the dynamic side, the behavior-milieu parts of a behavior setting, the synomorphs, have a specified degree of interdependence among themselves that is greater than their interdependence with parts of other behavior settings. These are the essential attributes of a behavior setting; the crucial terms will now be defined and elaborated (the comments refer to the italicized words). (1) A behavior setting consists of one or more **standing patterns** of behavior. Many nits of behavior have been identified: reflex, actone, action molar unit, and group activity are examples. A standing pattern of behavior is another behavior unit. It is a bounded pattern in the behavior of men, en masse. Examples in Midwest are a basketball game, a worship service, a piano lesson. A standing pattern of behavior is not a common behavior element among disparate behavior elements, such as the twang in Midwestern speech or the custom in small American towns of greeting strangers when they are encountered on the street. A standing pattern of behavior is a discrete behavior entity with univocal temporal-spatial coordinates; a basketball game, a worship service, or a piano lesson has, in each case, a precise and delimited position in time and space. Furthermore, a standing pattern of behavior is not a characteristic of the particular individuals involved; it is an extra-individual behavior phenomenon; it has unique characteristics that persist when the participants change."

[Barker, Roger G. Ecological Psychology. p. 28-29]
"The structural attributes of behavior settings are directly perceived. One sees that the behavior of the Saturday Night dance (ticket-taking, dancing, conversing, eating, playing musical instruments, etc.) occurs inside, not outside, the setting (of which the hall is part); one sees that the geographical arrangement of the chairs, the open floor area, the refreshment counter, the drums, etc., is congruent with the **pattern of behavior**. But the dynamic attributes of behavior settings, their internal unity, and the forces patterning persons, behavior, and objects into the shape and order required by the setting are indirectly apprehended. The evidence initially available to us on the dynamics of behavior settings will now be presented.
Influence of behavior settings upon the behavior of inhabitants. The influence of behavior settings upon behavior is exhibited in natural experiments that occur in Midwest. In these experiments, behavior settings

are the independent variable and the behavior of Midwest inhabitants the dependent variable. Data of one such experiment are presented in table 3.1, where some aspects of the behavior of the children of the second grade are summarized as they passed from one behavior setting to another during the school day. The same children exhibit these **different patterns** of behavior day after day; and the experiment is repeated each year with a new group, with the same results. The changes observed in the behavior of children as they change from one setting to another can only be ascribed to forces operating within the behavior settings."

[Ittelson, William H. and Proshansky, Harold M.   An Introduction to Environmental Psychology: Research Methods in Environmental Psychology. p. 214]

"Objections to experimental procedures, from the point of view of the environmentalists, derive from their emphasis on discrete behaviors rather than the whole man. Ideally, our interest in not in the analysis of isolated psychological functions but in the intact behaviors and experiences of people in relation to relevant physical settings. A methodology for environmental research must evolve out of the nature and characteristics of the phenomena it studies.   to the extent that such phenomena are complex, isolated variables cannot (an should not) be specified. Seeking relationships between intact physical settings and the ongoing integrated behaviors of individuals means relating a **patterned environment** to a sequenced **pattern of human activity**. Moreover, such relationships must be studied over extended periods of time. Finally, they become meaningful only in the context of the total environment-the social, cultural, and institutional systems that define the existence of modern man."

[Collins, John B. Perceptual Dimensions of Architectural Space Validated against Behavioral Criteria. p.11]

"The second category incorporates investigations into the social and interpersonal impact of various architectural considerations. The most common variables encountered in this category include number of interpersonal confrontations occasioned by various design considerations (usually traffic **patterns**), the number of friendships formed, studies involving parameters of 'personal space'."

[Winkel, G. H. and Sasanoff, R. An Approach to an Objective Analysis of Behavior in Architectural Space. p. 352-353]

"Movement through the museum was selected as the user-behavior of interest because it was possible to obtain highly reliable estimates of **movement patterns**; because movement was one variable which appeared to be more easily amenable to study in a simulation setting; because movement is one variable which may be influenced by the form and content of any kind of space; and because movement in the museum situation represents an exceedingly crucial aspect of user behavior operating to define a complete 'museum experience'. It should be noted that movement is not a single-dimensioned variable. In addition to specification of path, **movement patterns** will reveal the number of exhibits visited, the particular points on the floor which the visitor passes over, the elapsed time spent in motion or at rest, head movements and body orientation, etc. Thus movement can serve as a potentially rich user behavior."

"by drawing a line on the plan corresponding to the movement of the subject in the actual space."

"and the time spent at that point recorded. If for some reason the subject stopped in the middle of the floor."

[Winkel, G. H. and Sasanoff, R. An Approach to an Objective Analysis of Behavior in Architectural Space. p. 359]

"The first analysis made consisted of collations of the separate tracking maps into composite maps, which give an overview of the paths which the subjects followed in their museum experience. Each of the individual tracking maps was combined into a single map, representing the path behavior of the sample. The method of presentation which was utilized involved the breakdown of the composite maps in such a way that the **path behavior** of the sample becomes clearer."

APPENDIX K: EMPIRICAL

[Rapoport, Amos. History and Precedent in Environmental Design. p.205-206]

"**Need for an Empirical base**. One finds, in the archaeological literature, a commitment to an empirical content of any inferences, generalizations, hypotheses, and theories. There is, consequently, a commitment to and a concern with **empirical data**. One of the criteria distinguishing science and scholarship from other forms of human endeavor is the testing of ideas against empirical data. This is the case whatever the particular form of the ideas, models, or whatever. Thus, it is argued, even in the case of approaches that explicitly reject 'positivism' that the archaeological record is empirically constraining; that **the empirical data prevent the adoption of just any theoretical positions** (Hodder 1982a;cf. Bunge 1983; Jacob 1982). Hence, models are not completely speculative, and there is a continuous interplay of theory and data. All the papers or books that develop models or theory always explicitly and, in detail, apply them to the relevant bodies of evidence."

"Because the task of archaeology is now seen as that of **'decoding' the information** revealed by the **patterns present in the record**, it follows that discovering the data, describing them and classifying them are important, indeed essential steps. One must have an adequate empirical base."

"often the availability of a large and varied body of data suggests major developments, models, and theories-"

"The development of new approaches, in turn, leads to the collection of more, and more valid and relevant data."

"Once these become even partly available, a field can progress through the constant interaction of ideas, concepts, hypotheses and theories, and data. It follows that such laws, generalizations, and theories in archaeology must have **empirical content; they must refer to the real world**. This then also raises basic questions concerning the kind of empirical data that constitutes evidence for or against a given hypothesis"

"This literature presupposes that the link with **empirical data is essential**."

"**Positive evaluation**, that is, confirmation, is related to: 1. The empirical falsity of empirical predictions. Those hypotheses for which test implications are false are less preferable. It is useful to note that the recent discussions in philosophy of science on falsification suggests that this is rather more complicated than it seems. 2. The number of observational predictions supported. Other things being equal, the hypothesis with the greatest number of supporting observational predictions is preferred. 3. The variety and independence of observational predictions shown to be empirically true becomes the criterion, other things being equal (Smith, 1977, p. 613). Although 'independence' is a difficult notion and all the criteria present problems that Smith (1977, 1978) and the literature generally discuss, it would appear that the three criteria taken together strongly support my discussion earlier about the need for the largest and broadest bodies of evidence, the greatest number of relevant disciplines, agreement with data and theories accepted in other fields, and so on. Correcting misconceptions is always related to data. Even when reanalysis of already existing data is involved in the first instance, it usually demands new data in order to support the corrected view. Often, the original misconception is due to a 'superficial reading of limited historical sources' "

"Third, it uses a wide range of methods applied to a wide variety of evidence, including written sources (ethnohistory), ethnographic analogy, and archaeological data, emphasizing daily life."

[Collins, John B. Perceptual Dimensions of Architectural Space Validated against Behavioral Criteria. p. 16-18]

"Visual comprehension of architectural form has been based not on an **empirical understanding** of the user's perceptions, but rather on the designer's formalized intuitions deriving from various statements of an ideal. Little in the way of scaling of these terms has been attempted either with regard to an ideal image or to specific examples of architectural form. Disagreement among experts is apparent when terms are applied to physical referents. By using bipolar scales of attributes described in terms most frequently used by designers, consistency of descriptions was analyzed for both the ideal image and for specific examples of architectural form. Three specific aims of the experiments are discussed: (1) to develop a common vocabulary for describing environmental attributes, (2) to assess the relation between visual satisfaction and complexity, ambiguity, and novelty in a sample of existing environments, and (3) to develop a model which can be utilized by designer to produce the desired attributes (p. 20). A study seminar of graduate design students at the University of California at Berkeley, conducted by Kenneth Craik, produced and Environmental **Display Adjective Checklist** which was generated by the group of trained designers indicating an amount of agreement on dictionary terms A through K. The resulting pool of items yielded 169 checklist entries which could be used (according to these graduate students) to describe physical environment both in terms of its physicalistic attributes and its mood-affective attributes."

"It is when aesthetic questions become part of the public domain, affect the economics of public administration, and become questions of political debate that we require **objective measures** to settle differences of opinion. Even then the cost of the more accurate decision must be weighed against the consequences of failure. This kind of situation occurs to some extent in large architecture"

[Collins, John B. Perceptual Dimensions of Architectural Space Validated against Behavioral Criteria. p. 20]

"Since we have been dependent traditionally upon our **intuitive responses** for the manipulation of this physical world, not enough thought has been given to a more **empirical approach** towards the design methodology concerned with the visual manipulation of the environment."

"As **form creators** we must begin to look carefully at what is known about **human behavior**, insofar as it can be described by the social and behavioral sciences."

"we must begin to fill in the design equation with those **missing fragments** which can pattern themselves more closely into a truly human solution to the questions of environment."

"if we are to be responsible for the **total environment**, the human response to this environment must inspire the search for truth about what this **physical world** actually is."

[Barker, Roger G. Ecological Psychology. p.1-2]

"The descriptive, natural history, ecological phase of investigation has had a minor place in psychology, and this has seriously limited the science. Experimental procedures have revealed something about the laws of behavior, but they have not disclosed, nor can they disclose, how the variables of these laws are distributed across the types and conditions of men. Experimental work has produced a host of **'if...,then'** **statements**:   If a one-inch red cube is placed on a table before an eight-month old infant, then he will attempt to grasp the cube (Halverson, 1943).   If a person is frustrated, then he will exhibit aggressive and regressive behavior (Barker, Dembo, Lewin, 1941)."

"Psychology knows how people behave under the conditions of experiments and clinical procedures, but it knows little about the distribution of these and other conditions, and of their behavior resultants, outside of laboratories and clinics."

[Ittelson, William H. and Proshansky, Harold M.   An Introduction to Environmental Psychology: Research Methods in Environmental Psychology. p.232]

"A form of direct observation that does fit into real-world environments is **behavior mapping**.   Hence, we track the movements of people through existing physical settings and observe the kinds of behavior that occur in relation to these settings.   Where ecological psychology stresses the social activity of a locale, mapping seeks to identify the uses of space as a factor in ongoing behavior.   The two methods are complimentary rather than incompatible, for **the behavioral stream is always subject to the contingencies of its physical setting**. By making an accurate record of what activities take place where, mapping helps us study behavior in its functional relation to a particular environment.   Behavior will be enacted in accordance with the opportunities or limitations of the milieu in which it occurs.   By using mapping one avoids the difficulty of asking people to describe their reactions to an environment which is frequently inadequate; many people do not verbalize their experiences satisfactorily and they may also be unaware that any change in behavior is taking place.   The technique is a reliable one and rigorous enough so that the categories of behavior can be used as dependent variables within an experimental framework, yet without cluttering this framework by control interferences."

[Hall, Edward T. Handbook for Proxemic Research. p.3]

"**Proxemic observations** were made in **19 dimensions**:   (1) Posture   (2) **Body orientation**   (3) **Lateral displacement of bodies**   (4) **Change of orientation**   (5) **Change of distance**   (6) **Body distance**   (7) **Gestures: degree of movement**   (8) **Kinesis isomorphism**   (9) Affect: kind (10) Affect: intensity (11) **Eye behavior**   (12) Auditory code: number talking   (13) Auditory code: linguistic style   (14) Auditory code: voice loudness   (15) Auditory code: listening behavior   (16) Olfaction   (17) Thermal code (18) **Bodily involvement** (19) **Seeking avoiding touch**"

[Hall, Edward T. Handbook for Proxemic Research. p.57-62]

"**Body Orientation**: This scale describes the orientation of the subjects' bodies to each other." "The shoulders are the reference points to observe in deciding orientation."

"**Lateral Displacement of Bodies**: Refers to the amount of displacement on the body orientation scale (63). Record the degree to which the subjects are removed from the base positions. The displacements spectrum is amplified by adding increments of space to the basic displacement of the subjects;"

"**Change of Orientation**: This scale refers to change of body orientation between closed position, and open position (see Col. No. 63). Record as closing any movement toward a closed position, and as opening, any movement toward an open position. No movement, or movement which does not change or is not related to either open or closed position, should be recorded no change."

"**Change of Distance**: Record whether the subject is moving toward or away from the person with whom he is interacting."

"**Body Distance**: This scale measures the distance between the subjects, employing the body's own measuring rods; that is, the distances are based on what people can do with their arms, legs, and bodies, and are formulated according to four basic potential touching distances: (1) Body or head contact (2) Elbow's or forearm's length away (3) Full arm's length away (4) Within reach by stretching (body leaning, arm and leg extended)."

"**Gestures (Degree of Movement)**: This scale is used to record the degree to which the subject is gesturing or moving his body and its extremities."

"**Kinesic isomorphism**: This scale attempts to record the degree to which two people are mirroring each other's actions or body positions. This effect may be discovered by comparing the positions of both subjects' heads, hands, bodies, arms, legs, feet, etc."

"**Eye Behavior**: This scale refers to the gaze line. Record how the subject is looking at his interlocutor."

"**Bodily Involvement**: This scale records the kind or extent of physical contact between subjects-either actual or about to occur."

"Extensive body involvement includes such activities as pushing, shoving, necking, wrestling and making love. Holding hands or extremities also includes holding on to parts of clothing such as lapels, cuffs, skirt hems, etc."

"**Seeking or Avoiding Touching**: Regarding contact, subjects usually seek it, avoid it, or remain neutral. If Subject A is reaching to shake hands, he should be coded as 8 (seeking contact). If Subject B makes no move to take the offered hand, he should be coded as 2 (passively avoided contact). Two people passing each other on the street can seek each other out or avoid each other."

APPENDIX L: ANALYTICS

[Hall, Edward T. Handbook for Proxemic Research. p.22-26]

"**setting** (one aspect of context) is inextricably involved with behavior and that given a particular context, an **individual chooses (unconsciously)** which one of a number of behavioral repertoires is appropriate."

"Stated somewhat differently, **situational frames** (S/F's), and the **action chains** performed in the frames, apparently constitute the smallest meaningful complete components of culture."

"The point is that the linguistic codes, the clothes worn, the material surroundings, the type of association, the activity, the sex of the parties involved, and the temporal and spatial setting are all patterned, albeit often unconsciously, by culture. The entire situational frame functions under cultural constraints."

"**Primary activities** are also, archetypal and physiological, or common to all cultures. These might be termed nonsetting activities such as breathing. Nonsetting activities are contrasted with those that occur in settings, or for which settings exist, such as birth and death, eating and sleeping, excreting, sex and the like, all of which exist as kind of given in the human as well as the prehuman situation. **Secondary activities** are also, if not biologically based, at least widely shared among other species, but they do not have the imperative quality associated with primary activities. Secondary activities would include such things as grooming, washing, raising the young, maintenance of all types, learning and play, communicating and associating."

"The proxemicist's responsibility is primarily focused on the **setting and people's behavior in that setting**."

"All of the sets that go to make up a situational frame (time, space, situational dialects, and materials, that is, the microcultural setting, people and association, extensions including language, activities, as

well as the bisexual and learning aspects) are governed by the **laws of order, selection**, and **congruence**, particularly congruence (Hall 1959). As stated earlier high congruence equals a good performance in addition to all of the above."

"Situations follow either an **open or closed score**, are **high or low context**, and occur in a **public or private context**. All of these distinctions are important."

"a **score** can be anything from a simple shopping list to a musical score to a computer program. Some scores tend toward closedness and some are more open. **Success** in performance in a closed score requires the user to achieve the objectives as set down in the score-putting a man on the moon-with all that implies. One slip and the mission aborts. **Failure** when using an open score is to follow the score too closely because to do so inhibits the expression of individual and situational factors. The jazz or rock combo, if it is good, follows an open score."

"Closed scores are L/C, open scores are H/C."

"**The order law** (Hall 1959) applies- in fact, seems to dominate-the action chain."

"Indeed, virtually everything that living creatures do constitutes an action chain of some type."

"From the proxemicist's viewpoint, the importance of action chains is that not only is there a **beginning, fulfillment, and termination stage**, each broken down into a number of steps, but the **proxemic events** that must be recorded are determined by the sets or stages in the action chain."

"as one moves from one point to another in an action chain, there are either **subtle** or quite **obvious** shifts"

"Another important, highly relevant feature of the action chain is that there must be a certain type and amount of both **time and space**, as well as other **environmental features**, before it can be played out."

"The term 'action chain' can be misleading in that a chain of events is normally conceived as linear."

"The complex chains are played out following **innate** as well as **learned** paradigms in which responses are released alternately and in sequence in the two partied until the goal is reached. Sexual intercourse would be an example of a complex chain in which many of the steps are pre-programmed, but modified by culture."

[Hall, Edward T. Handbook for Proxemic Research. p.102]

"It is a mistake to limit studies such as this one to a single statistic. Commenting on **statistics**-this is the Western world's way of validating what sensitive observers discover in a fraction of the time. The statistical treatment, however, does suggest new observations and may even help to tell us what to pay attention to."

Future workers are encouraged to experiment and to innovate, for everything new that was tried has taught us something."

[Ittelson, William H. and Proshansky, Harold M. An Introduction to Environmental Psychology: Research Methods in Environmental Psychology. p.210-211]

"**Holistic Research**. In this procedure the objective is not the study of selected environmental variable, but rather **the relationships which exist among these variables as part of a complex situation**. Broadly speaking, this design is qualitative, seeking the underlying themes of a situation rather than the relationships existing between isolated variables. 'Holistic research takes as its problem the nature of the total system rather than of a particular process within the situation.' (Weiss 1968:343) Like experimental research, it also has a set of procedures enabling the researcher to check the validity of his assumptions."

"**The Field Study**. Unlike survey research the field study uses existing data. For this reason it is often called an ex post facto method. Demographic information, such as government statistics, medical records, and the like, comprise the raw material, over which, or course, the investigator has no control. Field studies correlate this social, physical, and psychological data in an effort **to find relevant associations that may indicate a causa relationship among specific variables**."

"**Exploratory Research**. Like the holistic model this approach can be used to study complex environments such as cities or ethnic communities. However, the material gathered this way is more likely **to be quantified and correlated into possible sets of significant relationships**. It says, in effect, 'Let's look at the situation and see what characteristics are suggested for further study.' Thus, in practice, exploratory research is frequently preliminary to a more precisely formulated and narrowly focused design in which, it is hoped, certain causal relationships can be tested."

"All research is simply the gathering and interpretation of information. It is the point of view behind the study - the objectives of the investigation - that determines the most suitable overall procedure."

"Many research procedures rely heavily on the observation of behavior by the investigator."

"he might **observe unobtrusively** and make an exact record of his observations by using a **camera** or tape recorder. He may then systematize or **map his observations** according to predetermined **categories of interest or time segments**. Sometimes he will use a confederate to stimulate certain kinds of behavior he wants to study. Additional techniques especially pertinent to environmental research include simulation of selected aspects of an environment, cognitive mapping, and gaming. In **simulation** one attempts to create a mock environment in order to predict behavior in a comparable real environment. **Cognitive mapping** indirectly reveals something about an individual's behavior by comparing his mental image of an environment to that which actually exists. **Gaming** uses simulated situations or processes, as well as environments, in an effort both to elicit behavior traits which the individual may not always be aware of and to acquaint

the player with the complexities of the many environments with which he may have contact."

[Ittelson, William H. and Proshansky, Harold M. An Introduction to Environmental Psychology: Research Methods in Environmental Psychology. p.218-221]

"If you want to know how a person stands on a question, ask him. Of course, he may not be aware of the real nature of his opinions; except for conspicuous deviations from what is usual, for example, new settings may influence the behavior of the person with **little or no conscious awareness on his part**. What he is unaware of he clearly cannot report, although, in fact, **his behavior may have changed**. Possibly, he will also be biased: what a person thinks about something is filtered through his prejudices, hopes, and expectations."

"Because people are not always aware of the effect a setting has on their actions, the survey approach, in some instances, may be quite inappropriate."

[Ittelson, William H. and Proshansky, Harold M. An Introduction to Environmental Psychology: Research Methods in Environmental Psychology. p.222-224]

"In **holistic and exploratory research** such material is evaluated largely on the basis of personal judgment, with statistical formulations playing a secondary role."

"When physical objects are the components of an experiment this is relatively easy. Distance, weight, size of object, and the time necessary for a given event to take place can be expressed in quantitative terms; interaction among the variables-which is the purpose of the experiment-is measured empirically and described statistically."

"A number of techniques are used to make such information more clearly interpretable. The most commonly employed, and the one discussed here, is **factor analysis**. In essence, factor analysis identifies those items or attributes that can be grouped (hence studied) together, rather than separately, because of a particular property or 'factor,' they share in common. Ideally, it limits the number of variables which must be dealt with and in this sense simplifies data analysis. This affinity grouping is done **statistically** by ascertaining the nature of the correlations among the items included in the study."

"**Objective physical and geographical measures**. The topological attributes of a setting, both as entities and in relation to one another, are subject to measurement. They have size, weight, shape, color, and temperature, and are separated from other entities by exact distances. These are the verifiable physical qualities of an environment."

"**Sequential notational systems**. (Thiel 1970). These describe reactions to an environment as experienced by an observer moving through it. Certain objects and surfaces constitute **'space-establishing elements'** which orient one's movements through a setting. The architect's elevations, plans, and perspectives together constitute a form of notational system."

[Ittelson, William H. and Proshansky, Harold M. An Introduction to Environmental Psychology: Research Methods in Environmental Psychology. p.231]

"Observation of an ongoing series of activities made at specific intervals is known as **time-sampling**. By shifting the emphasis one can also measure the various occurrences irrespective of their time span. This is known as **event-sampling**."

[Ittelson, William H. and Proshansky, Harold M. An Introduction to Environmental Psychology: Research Methods in Environmental Psychology. p.234]

"reproduce a simulated or mock environment and then observe the individual's response to it. **A scale model.**"

"By looking at the model and evaluating our **reaction to it**, we decide, for example, whether or not we think it is attractive or whether it will suit our needs."

"It has the further advantage that it can precede and therefore act as a guide to changing the real environment."

"Recently techniques have been devised in which the relationships generated by the environment are used rather than a realistic reproduction of it. In other words, our model need not resemble the real object; it is important, however, that its components operate as though in a real-life situation. 'Successful **simulation** requires only that one be able to reproduce the system under study as accurately as possible without actually employing the system itself."

"It **abstracts** what are believed to be the salient aspects of the real-world system and replicates them for purposes of study."

[Alp, Ahmet Vefik. An Experimental Study of Aesthetic Response to Geometric Configurations of Architectural Space. p.151-156]

"The objective of our research was to use systematically **manipulated physical/visual aspects** of architectural space to determine their **'aesthetic-emotional effects**.' All other perceptual variables were kept constant in order to detect possible causal relationships."

"Describing **a list of adjectives** that represents and describes the aesthetic dimension of architecture was my first step in devising the measuring instrument."

"I compiled **scales** from those that previous research had established as representing the aesthetic dimension of the built environment (Table 2)."

"a final list of 26 adjectives was created (Fig. 1). Instead of using **bipolar scales** where two contrasted or antonymic adjectives delimit the end-points, **a single adjective** was employed to represent each scale to avoid any confusion that might result from the ambiguity of antonyms. While scales used to describe the perception of physical properties and

that express a range such as light to dark' appear to lie on a **linear** continuum, this may not be the case for emotive scales such as 'kind to cruel,' which seems to contain several **latent** scales, including 'kind to not-kind' and 'cruel to not-cruel' (23). We used the findings from various studies to establish an aesthetic-dimension structure that would be valid cross-culturally and cross-architecturally."

"The **independent variable** in this experiment consisted of three geometrical configurations of architectural space: a rectangle, a triangle and a circle."

"The three models simulated fictitious office spaces, standardized for space and furniture arrangements."

"Respondents were encouraged to make more natural eye-level observations using the window openings at the perimeter walls."

"The models, including their furniture, were built by the same craftsperson using the same materials. Color, texture and the quality of craft were, therefore, identical."

"The use of **primary forms** was intended to control confounding effects from the differing visual complexity of the three models. The primary shapes have been demonstrated to be perceived easily and rapidly and to possess the same degree of visual information and simplicity/complexity."

"the independent variable conditions were equated on all 'Gestalt factors of formal organization.' "

"The correlation of results elicited using **scale models** and **full-scale environments** was thoroughly investigated."

"The analysis indicated that observers tend to be even more constant on assessments of scale models than of full-size rooms."

"of the three geometric conditions, at least two differed significantly."

"**triangular** versus **rectangular** conditions and **rectangular** versus **circular** conditions yielded more significant differences (p<.01) than did **triangular** versus **circular** conditions"

"**circular** space-system had the highest score of positive adjectives,"

"the **rectangular** space organization was the least preferred one."

"unfamiliar geometric organizations, specifically circular and triangular layouts, are preferred over right-angle intersections - implying that people, including architects, adapt to the familiar space configurations, and consequently are attracted to original and novel spatial relations."

APPENDIX M: The study of a Design Process: Refinement of Perceived Form and Space

[Schlueb, Matthew Thomas. Independent Study: Thesis Research. p.2-34]

*In the fall semester of 1993, an independent study (thesis research) was undertaken within the Industrial Design Department, School of Art and Design, Pratt Institute; under the direction of **Martin Skalski**, **Deborah Gans**, and **William Fogler**.   The results of the study are recorded in the following document; expanding on the design process used to create the unified forms that were introduced into a site on the Pratt Institute campus.   This document consists of three sections: the original statement of proposed study, a description of the design process studied, and three examples of the 'form-space' studies.*

SECTION I: STATEMENT OF PROPOSED STUDY: (original submission date: 93.7.1)

The perception of form is the creation of space; manipulated and adjusted by one's individual senses and memory.

In pursuing an independent study in the Industrial Design Department, I am interested in the physical and perceptual qualities of form and space in relation to the human senses and memory. During the study I will use the methodology and approach to teaching employed within this department. I feel the understanding of visual perception from an abstract and experiential viewpoint will strengthen my design abilities when brought back to an architectural perspective.

The goal of this study is to develop a design process; through study of the characteristics and operating devices that are intrinsic to any form, by isolating and adjusting three-dimensional qualities of form and space. The use of interactive criticism with my advisor on analysis models and sketches, will lead to the finalized production of a Model demonstrating the design process of formal and spatial relationships and their levels of responsibility each characteristic acquires and operates within.

SECTION II: THE DESIGN PROCESS:

The influences of activated space on the occupant, can be studied by the controlled continual refining sedimentation ('fine tuning') of relational forms perceived by its occupant.

In the study of architecture and the creation of space, there must be an understanding of the occupant and an assumption made of the function of space. The occupant's responses depend on the physical and psychological realms of its environment. The psychological necessities are subtle in character, requiring sensitive attention. The architectural function of space, is simply the adjustment of perceived form and space, in order to stimulate the relational and proxemic behaviors of the human body and mind. The structures of the relationship between the occupant and the architectural space are rooted in the characteristics and operating devices of the human condition. Human proxemic behavior is more than a conscious intellect, rather a combination of reason and reflex. A study of proxemic reflexes aside from conceptualized reasoning will conclude in an understanding of the human condition, the architectural spatial condition, and the relational dialogue between the two. To become more sensitive to that dialogue, a bridging of the human condition and architectural condition is unavoidable. Space that has been designed with sensitivity to proxemic behavior (i.e., space reacting to human occupation and occupants reacting to the spatial form), will result in a space that accentuates the dialogue between the occupant and the occupied, creating a more sensitized and enveloping context.

In the early phases of the creation of form and space, the subconscious mind is used predominately, with judgment and adjustment sensitivity based on an internalized focus of intuition. Multiple 'influences' (design characteristics within a form) found within the modeled space are weighed and processed while relating all 'influences' simultaneously. Once these 'influences' fuse together into a relational understanding of the character and intensity of each 'influence', the context as a whole begins to solidify in the foreconscious mind. The later phase of the creation process, taking place with a foreconscious awareness, is limited to adjusting one or two 'influences' at a time, in relation to the human figure within the modeled space. Foreconscious awareness of the direct and literal relationship under study, with the added subconscious intuition, enables the process of refinement of each 'influence' to the most effective position. This dialectic condition of the subconscious and foreconscious minds is exploited to benefit the creation process, through a method of each mind addressing its own strengths and relying on the other mind to handle any weakness.

The 'fine tuning' (adjustment and refinement) of an original form and group of forms in three-dimensional space, was accomplished with attention to surface and proximity, density and gravitation, scale and relationship, character and articulation. The earliest part of the study involved the analysis of a series of two-dimensional and three-dimensional spaces, with respect to their juxtaposition and enveloping (an 'activated' space enclosing its occupant) qualities. Next, was the selection of several typical spatial conditions on the Pratt campus to be studied with the introduction of articulated forms sensitized to soften and humanize the existing rigid and sterile threshold surfaces. Finally, the spatial conditions were narrowed to one, a transitional space: an entry hall, selected to focus the study at a deeper level of human circulation and proxemic behavioral patterns in context with the articulated forms.

The process began by identifying the primary 'gesture' (a form's 'influence' on a space) within the space, which is then studied through a refinement of the space's form and threshold relationships. Once the primary 'gesture' is improved upon and unified (most effective refined adjustment), it is broken down into two or three secondary 'gestures' which when considered together make up the primary 'gesture' of the space. These secondary 'gestures' are refined in the same manner as the first and then placed back within the larger context, to study their new 'influences' and effects on the primary 'gesture' of the space. This process of breaking down 'gestures' into secondary 'gestures' to be studied at a reduced scale, then to be re-introduced within the larger context and studied at an additive scale, can be repeated indefinitely to a desired level of refinement in 'gesture'.

The study of each 'gesture' is accomplished through a 'comparative modeling' technique that focuses on one adjustment at a time, without changing the character of the larger context. The success of this 'comparative modeling' is dependent on an ability to recognize and qualify the implications of the single adjustment. In order to accomplish this, two identical models of the spatial context are used, placing the attention of study on the subtle difference between the two resulting from the adjustment. Once the two are compared with each other, one can be determined to be more effective at defining the desired character of the space, thereby creating an 'improved' condition. The development of an 'improved' condition aids in understanding the 'influences' and intensities resulting from each adjustment. An adjustment begins with a movement of a single form to the extreme thresholds within the character of the space and then focused to the most distinct and effective location, defining and punctuating the desired 'gesture'. After the 'gestures' are improved upon to their most effective spatial arrangement, the introduction of a human scale figure is used to locate and identify envelopment thresholds. This human figure is moved from place to place in small and subtle increments to measure the changes in the activated space (a defined envelope of space, implied by 'gestured' forms) and proxemic sensitivities; resulting in further adjustments and refinement of the 'gestures' in reaction to the human scale figure intervention. Through the use of the human figure, the perception of the thresholds and densities of the activated space can be sharpened, to complete the refinement process.

Professor Martin Skalski, from the Industrial Design Department, guided the design process used in the derivation and adjustment of the form and spatial intervention into the campus site. Professor Deborah Gans, from the Undergraduate Architecture Department, acted as a critic and intervened on behalf of the School of Architecture in this study. Professor William Fogler, from the School of Art and Design, was consulted at several points during the design process for perceptual and critical insights.

SECTION III: 'FORM-SPACE' STUDIES:

Documented in this section are three examples of the form-space studies undertaken during the Independent Study. However, before they are outlined, there is a need to define some of the terminology used by the Industrial Design Department, for discussion and criticism of these studies.

FORM: A three-dimensional solid; with scale, surface, and identity. While most 'forms' in these studies are a single, physically-independent object, there are a few cases where multiple 'forms' are combined to produce a single object.

GESTURE: An accenting characteristic or focal point found within a 'form'; suggesting a movement, direction, or unique quality within that 'form'. The 'gesture' of a 'form' defines the influence a 'form' has on the related space. A 'gesture' does not refer to the traditional sense of the word: an anatomical movement; except in a metaphoric sense, as extended to an inanimate 'form': a projection of a 'form' onto a related space.

ACTIVATED SPACE: A type of space; with a threshold defined by one or more 'gestured forms'. Space becomes 'activated' when its thresholds are perceivable, due to the implications of the related 'gestured forms'. The perception of 'gestured forms' generally attracts or repels the occupant, however once perceived, the space has become 'activated'.

INACTIVE SPACE: A type of space; with no defining characteristics or related 'gestured forms' (the antithesis of 'activated space'). Space becomes 'inactive' when it doesn't have any self-defined thresholds and is only defined by the thresholds of other spaces.

ENVELOP: A characteristic of space; defining threshold, engagement, and enclosure. When a 'gestured form' defines an 'activated space' related to that 'form', the 'gestured form' will engage, enclose, and 'envelop' any object or human body found within that 'activated space'. 'Envelopment' establishes a proxemic relationship between the 'enveloping' form and space, to the 'enveloped' body or object within that space.

DETACH: A characteristic of space; defining isolation, exclusion, and independence (the antithesis of 'envelop'). A body or object becomes 'detached' when it is found outside all defined 'activated spaces' of 'gestured forms'. 'Detachment' results when there are no proxemic relationships existing between the 'detached' body or object and any 'enveloping' forms and spaces. A 'detached' body or object can only exist within 'inactive space'.

ORIGINAL CONDITION: A subconscious prototype; the first of a series. An initial physical condition, in 'gestured form(s)' and 'activated space(s)', responding to a set of initial impressions based on relational qualities.

IMPROVED CONDITION: A foreconscious derivation of an 'original condition'; arrived at through refining adjustments of the related characteristics between the 'gestured forms' and 'activated spaces'. The condition becomes an 'improvement' over the 'original condition' when it is more effective at defining a desired direction of development.

UNIFIED CONDITION: A finalized derivation of an 'improved condition'; arrived at through a sedimentation in refining adjustments of the related characteristics between the 'gestured forms' and 'activated spaces'. The condition becomes 'unified' when it has reached its most effective definition of a desired direction of development.

EXAMPLE I: ONE FORM ADJUSTMENT WITH TWO SPACES:

This form-space study was one of the introductory studies in the Independent Study, dealing with two gestured forms, adjustment of one of the two gestured forms, and two activated spaces. The primary gestured form, the larger curved vertical surface in the upper right corner of the contextual plane, defines the larger activated space. The secondary gestured form, the smaller curved vertical surface in the center of the contextual plane, defines the smaller activated space. (Fig. 5) The two activated spaces were composed in relation to each other; the primary activated space is to be 'passive' in relation to the secondary activated space which is to be 'active'. Since both spaces are by definition 'activated spaces', the differentiation between the two is in their relative quantity and quality of 'activation' to each other. Because there is an overlap of spaces in the lower center of the contextual plane, the secondary activated space is perceived to be more 'activated' then the primary activated space, by relation more 'passive.' (Fig. 5)

The original condition, as described in the previous paragraph, establishes two well defined spaces both in front and behind the secondary gestured form. However, with closer study, it is realized that the two spaces are very closely balanced in their levels of 'activation' of space, once they are compared to the human scale figure placed within their respective spaces. (Fig. 1 and 2) The degree in envelopment of the human figures when placed within the spaces is very similar, resulting in a perception of two balanced 'activated' spaces. This condition needs adjustment, since the desired result as stated in the previous paragraph, was to offset the balance of these two spaces, making one more 'active' then the other. To accomplish this, the movement of the secondary gestured form from its original condition, backward and to the left on the contextual plane, enlarges the overlapping space in the lower center of the contextual plane. (Fig. 3 and 4) This movement of the secondary gestured form in the improved condition, transforms the perception of the secondary activated space by using the primary gestured form to aid in defining the perimeter dimension at the right of the contextual plane. (Fig. 6) Since the positioning of the secondary gestured form in the original condition did not allow as much influence of the primary gestured form in the perception of the secondary activated space (Fig. 5), the perceivable overlap between the two spaces was not as effective as in the improved condition. Once the adjustment was made to the secondary gestured form, the improved condition was studied to check the relative envelopment of the human scale figures in the two new spaces. (Fig. 7 and 8) The secondary activated space clearly dominates the improved condition, almost to the point of eliminating any sense of space in the primary activated space. This condition pushes the primary activated space beyond 'passive' and into tight or claustrophobic. A tight or claustrophobic spatial context would suggest an entirely different proxemic vocabulary in relation to an 'active' and 'passive' vocabulary found in a more open and breathable spatial context.   Because of this reason, this particular study was kept relatively simple by steering away from tight or claustrophobic spaces, and keeping the two spaces both in a open and breathable spatial context, to ease the comparison process.

As a result, there was a need to adjust the improved condition, to eliminate the tight or claustrophobic sense in the primary activated space.   The movement of the secondary gestured form from the improved condition, forward and slightly to the right, to the refined unified condition resolved this problem. (Fig. 9 and 10)   By opening up the primary activated space in the unified condition, it is transformed from a tight or claustrophobic space to a 'passive' space, in relation to the more 'active' space in the original condition. (Fig. 11 and 12)   The adjustment of the secondary gestured form has reached a refinement point of sedimentation, a unified condition, bridging a relationship between the two activated spaces, with one becoming more 'active' and the other more 'passive'.   The secondary gestured form in the unified condition, establishes a direct proxemic relationship with the lower right edge of the primary gestured form (Fig. 14); a relationship that does not exist in the original condition (Fig. 13) but exists with a much larger portion of the primary gestured form in the improved condition. (Fig. 6)   By reducing the proxemic relationship down from the lower half of the primary gestured form in the improved condition (Fig. 6) to the edge of the primary gestured form in the unified condition (Fig. 14), the entire surface of the primary gestured form could now be dedicated solely to the primary activated space. (Fig. 9 and 10) In the unified condition, the primary gestured form's surface defines a 'passive' space, while the primary gestured form's edge, with the secondary gestured form, define an 'active' space. (Fig. 13 and 14)

The series of conditions: original, improved, and unified, were the result of many adjustments and subtle refinements between these three conditions.   The study is clarified by presenting only the three most explicit examples of the primary intermediate points. It is important to point out that the three conditions found here, in relation to each other, are not a true reflection of the many and subtle adjustments studied, but were selected for documentation to facilitate the illustration of the design process under study.

FIGURE 1: ORIGINAL CONDITION; HUMAN FIGURE IN REAR

Human scale figure enveloped by the primary activated space. In this condition, the primary activated space is pushed back to the rear of the contextual plane (Fig. 5), the primary gestured form is separated from the front half of the plane, both as a result of the secondary gestured form located so far forward.

FIGURE 2: ORIGINAL CONDITION; HUMAN FIGURE IN FRONT

Human scale figure enveloped by the secondary activated space. In this condition, the secondary activated space is independently located in the front of the contextual plane (Fig. 5), resulting from the secondary gestured form being visually separated from the primary gestured form's influences.

FIGURE 3: ORIGINAL CONDITION; BOTH HUMAN FIGURES

Both human scale figures are enveloped by the activated spaces, related to their respective gestured forms. Both activated spaces are equally balanced in their visually perceivable 'active' character. Since, the secondary gestured form is located forward, the primary activated space opens up, eliminating any 'passive' character.

FIGURE 4: IMPROVED CONDITION; BOTH HUMAN FIGURES

The secondary gestured form is adjusted, moving back and to the left of its original condition. This closes off the primary activated space in the rear, shifting the influence of the primary gestured form to the front with the secondary gestured form, detaching both human figures from the newly concentrated activated spaces. (Fig. 6)

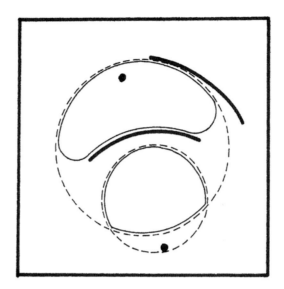

FIGURE 5: ORIGINAL CONDITION; ILLUSTRATION

This plan view illustrates the balance of the two spaces sensed as 'active'; graphically represented as thin lines. The thin dashed lines represent the enveloping space that becomes activated by their related gestures form. Note that in this condition, the influence of the primary gestured form does not extend down to reach the lower human figure.

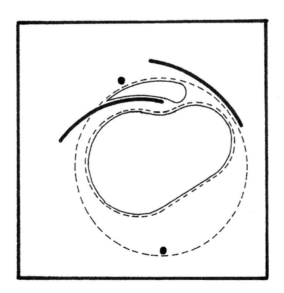

FIGURE 6: IMPROVED CONDITION; ILLUSTRATION

This plan view illustrates the shift in the primary activated space, from a balanced condition of two 'active' spaces to an unbalanced condition of 'tight' vs 'active' spaces, shown as thin lines. Influence of the primary gestured form creates a concentration of space extending out and to the right of the secondary activated space, detaching the human figure.

FIGURE 7: IMPROVED CONDITION; HUMAN FIGURE IN REAR

Human scale figure detached from the primary activated space. The adjustment of the secondary gestured form has shifted the primary activated space toward the front of the contextual plane, resulting in a detachment of that space from the human figure. (Fig. 6) The two activated spaces are unbalanced with each other.

FIGURE 8: IMPROVED CONDITION; HUMAN FIGURE IN FRONT

Human scale figure detached from the secondary activated space, however, it also has a subtle envelopment from the shifted primary activated space. The adjustment has pulled the secondary activated space away from the human figure, as a concentrated 'active' space which is dominate and over the rear 'tight' space. (Fig. 6)

FIGURE 9: IMPROVED CONDITION; BOTH HUMAN FIGURES

Both human scale figures are detached by the activated spaces, related to their respective gestured forms. In this condition, the two activated spaces are unbalanced; the front space is an open 'active' space and the rear space is a 'tight' space. Refinement is needed to enable a visual perception of the rear space as more 'passive'.

FIGURE 10: UNIFIED CONDITION; BOTH HUMAN FIGURES

The secondary gestured form is refined to a unified condition, moving forward and slightly to the right of the improved condition. This adjustment reaffirms the primary gestured form to the rear, primary activated space, bringing that space from a previous 'tight' condition to a more open, understated activated, 'passive' condition.

FIGURE 11: ORIGINAL CONDITION; BOTH HUMAN FIGURES

Both human scale figures are enveloped by the activated spaces, related to their respective gestured forms. Both activated spaces are equally balanced in their visually perceived 'active' character. However, there is a need for some refined adjustment, since the desired result of this study is to create relative spaces: 'active' and 'passive'.

FIGURE 12: UNIFIED CONDITION; BOTH HUMAN FIGURES

Both human scale figures are enveloped by the activated spaces, related to their respective gestured forms. The adjustment of the secondary gestured form, from the previous improved condition, engages the primary gestured form's lower right edge to create a separation between the rear 'passive' space and the front 'active' space.

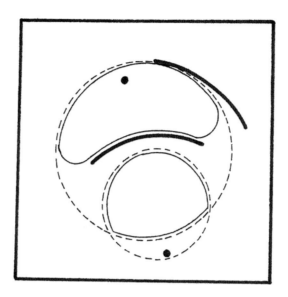

FIGURE 13: ORIGINAL CONDITION; ILLUSTRATION

This plan view illustrates the balance of the two spaces sensed as 'active'; graphically represented as thin lines. The thin dashed lines represent the enveloping space that becomes activated by their related gestured form. Note that in this condition, the influence of the primary gestured form does not extend down to reach the lower human figure.

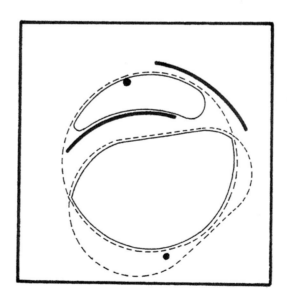

FIGURE 14: UNIFIED CONDITION; ILLUSTRATION

This plan view illustrates the shift in the primary activated space, from a balanced condition of an 'active' space to a slightly subordinate 'passive' space. Influence from the primary gestured form's edge, with the secondary gestured form, create a concentrated space in the front center of the contextual plane, that envelops the lower human figure.

EXAMPLE II: TWO FORM VARIATIONS WITH TWO LINE SEGMENTS:

This form-space study was one of the intermediate studies in the Independent Study, dealing with two gestured forms, adjustment of both of the gestured forms, and a three-dimensional activated space. The primary gestured form, the darker line segment in the front right of the contextual plane, defines the primary gesture of the activated space. The secondary gestured form, the lighter line segment in the top left of the contextual plane, defines the secondary gesture of the activated space. (Fig. 15) The two gestured forms (the two line segments), when combined create an activated space; to be enhanced by the composed relationship between the two gestures. The enhancement of the activated space, documented here, is a process of many variations and adjustments defining the desired character. The presentation of several of these variations and adjustments in the refinement of the activated space, provides an example of how the process evolved. It is important to point out that the conditions found here, are only a few intermediate steps in the refinement process, not the entire evolution or the resulting unified condition.

The original condition establishes a defined space between and around the two gestured line segments; the primary line segment horizontal and parallel to the contextual plane (wooden base), and the secondary line segment at a diagonal (approximately thirty degrees off the contextual plane) and a skewed angle to the other line segment. (Fig. 15)   The activated space is divided into two halves by the lower end of the secondary line segment, while the desired effect is for a single enhanced activated space.   The first two variations to the original condition, take the character of the activated space in opposite directions, for comparison.   The first variation involves the movement of the primary line segment in a small clockwise revolution. (Fig. 15 and 16)   The second variation is a movement of the secondary line segment in a slight clockwise revolution. (Fig. 17 and 18)   The first variation makes the division of the activated space much more defined and severe, with the focus of attention on the narrow gap between the end of the secondary line segment and the middle of the primary line segment.   The second variation, in contrast to the first, opens that narrow gap to create a single activated space; with a subtle focus of attention on the twist in the space as it moves over the rear of the primary line segment, implied by the raised end of the secondary line segment as it cantilevers over the other line segment.   After comparison of these two variations, the first variation is found to be an improvement off of the original condition, if the desired effect is to be the definition of the two divided spaces.   However, the second variation is the preferred improvement, since the definition of a single activated space is desired for this study.   Even though the character of the original condition is lost in the secondary variation, it is a necessity in order to accomplish the refinement of a single activated space.   Therefore, the second variation is taken as the refinement of the original condition in the pursuit of the desired effect; and is now considered the improved condition (Fig. 18, 19, and 21), from which further adjustments are made.

The first two variations to the improved condition, take the character of the activated space in similar directions, for comparison.   The first variation off of the improved condition, involves the slight rotation of the secondary line segment in a clockwise movement. (Fig. 19 and 20)   By doing this, the space that twists over the rear of the primary line segment is enhanced, through the increased relationship between the rear primary line segment and the cantilevered end of the secondary line segment.   In contrast to that variation, the second variation off of the improved condition involves the lowering of the secondary line segment closer to the contextual plane without any change in rotation or angle. (Fig. 21 and 22)   This movement narrows the space between the two line segments, making a clearer relationship and enhancing the activated space.   In the case of these two variations from the improved condition, both adjustments improve the activated space toward the desired effect, since they both maintain the initial character of the improved condition.   These variations are both useful, unlike the two variations from the original condition, in which only one was useful and the other had to be dropped. Therefore, since both of these new variations are useful, there is a desire to combine the improvement qualities from both into one single improvement.

The first variation from the improved condition, enhances the activated space through the additional twisting of the space between the two line segments. The second variation from the improved condition, enhances the activated space through the tightening of the space between the two line segments. The combination of the enhancements from both variations into a 'new combined' improved condition will enable further refinements and adjustments from a single comparative condition. The combination of the first variation from the improved condition into the 'new combined' improved condition, is visible in the cantilevered twist of the secondary line segment. (Fig. 23 and 24) The combination of the second variation from the improved condition into the 'new combined' improved condition, is visible in the tighten distance between the two line segments. (Fig. 25 and 26) Therefore, both variations are taken as the refinements of the improved condition in the pursuit of the desired effect; and is now considered the 'new combined' improved condition (Fig. 24 and 26), from which further adjustments are made.

The series of conditions: original, improved, and 'new combined' improved, in addition to the variations of adjustments and refinements involved in the improvement process; were the result of many smaller and more subtle movements that were not documented here. The removal of these smaller and more subtle movements in the documentation process, was done to simplify and clarify the study, presenting just a sample of two different results (two variations in opposite directions of an original condition and two variations in similar directions of an improved condition) at an intermediate point within this particular study. Therefore, it is important to point out that the three conditions found here, in relation to each other, are not a true reflection of the subtlety in the adjustments studied, but were selected for documentation to facilitate the illustration of the design process under study.

FIGURE 15: ORIGINAL CONDITION

A defined space between and around the two gestured line segments. The activated space is divided into two halves by the lower end of the secondary line segment, while the desired effect is for a single enhanced activated space. This condition provides a base to derive variations of adjustments and refinements.

FIGURE 16: FIRST VARIATION FROM ORIGINAL CONDITION

The movement of the primary line segment (the lower right wooden rod) in a small clockwise revolution. This adjustment makes the division of the activated space much more defined and severe, with the focus of attention on the narrow gap between the end of the secondary line segment and the middle of the primary line segment.

FIGURE 17: ORIGINAL CONDITION

A defined space between and around the two gestured line segments. The activated space is divided into two halves by the lower end of the secondary line segment, while the desired effect is for a single enhanced activated space. This condition provides a base to derive variations of adjustments and refinements.

FIGURE 18: SECOND VARIATION FROM ORIGINAL CONDITION

IMPROVED CONDITION: The movement of the secondary line segment (the upper left wooden rod) in a slight clockwise revolution. This adjustment opens the narrow gap to create a single activated space, with a subtle focus of attention on the twist in the space as it moves over the rear of the primary line segment.

FIGURE 19: IMPROVED CONDITION

SECOND VARIATION FROM ORIGINAL CONDITION: A defined space between and around the two gestured line segments, improved from the original condition with the opening of the space in the mid section. The desired effect with the character of a single activated space is now installed in the improved condition.

FIGURE 20: FIRST VARIATION FROM IMPROVED CONDITION

The movement of the secondary line segment in a slight clockwise rotation. This adjustment enhances the space that twists over the rear of the primary line segment, through the increased engagement of the relationship between the cantilevered end of the secondary line segment and the rear of the primary line segment.

FIGURE 21: IMPROVED CONDITION

SECOND VARIATION FROM ORIGINAL CONDITION: A defined space between and around the two gestured line segments, improved from the original condition with the opening of the space in the mid section. The desired effect with the character of a single activated space is now installed in the improved condition.

FIGURE 22: SECOND VARIATION FROM IMPROVED CONDITION

The movement of the secondary line segment closer to the contextual plane. This adjustment enhances the space that narrows between the two line segments, through the clearer relationship resulting from a tighter proximity between the primary and secondary line segments.

FIGURE 23: FIRST VARIATION FROM IMPROVED CONDITION

The movement of the secondary line segment in a slight clockwise rotation. This adjustment enhances the space that twists over the rear of the primary line segment, through the increased engagement of the relationship between the cantilevered end of the secondary line segment and the rear of the primary line segment.

FIGURE 24: 'NEW COMBINED' IMPROVED CONDITION

COMBINATION OF TWO VARIATIONS FROM IMPROVED CONDITION: A defined space between and around the two gestured line segments, improved from the improved condition with the twisting and tightening of the space between the two line segments; an enhanced relationship of gestured forms in the activated space.

FIGURE 25: SECOND VARIATION FROM IMPROVED CONDITION

The movement of the secondary line segment closer to the contextual plane. This adjustment enhances the space that narrows between the two line segments, through the clearer relationship resulting from a tighter proximity between the primary and secondary line segments.

FIGURE 26: 'NEW COMBINED' IMPROVED CONDITION

COMBINATION OF TWO VARIATIONS FROM IMPROVED CONDITION: A defined space between and around the two gestured line segments, improved from the improved condition with the twisting and tightening of the space between the two line segments; an enhanced relationship of gestured forms in the activated space.

EXAMPLE III: THREE FORM ADJUSTMENTS WITH THREE SPACES:

This form-space study was one of the advanced studies in the Independent Study, dealing with three gestured forms, adjustment of all three gestured forms, and three activated spaces. The primary gestured form, the longer, low curved rectangular surface in the upper right corner of the contextual plane, defines the primary activated space. The secondary gestured form, the taller, narrow curved rectangular surface in the upper left corner of the contextual plane, defines the secondary activated space. The dependent gestured form, the curved rectangular surface with one corner angled off in the lower right corner of the contextual plane, defines the dependent activated space. (Fig. 29) The three activated spaces were composed in relation to each other, to be enhanced by the adjustment and refinement in the proxemics nature of the three gestured forms. The desired effect in this study is to maintain activated space in all three spaces, while attempting to balance the character and relationship among the spaces and gestured forms.

To begin this study, three independent original conditions were created to compare and select the best condition. The first original condition turned the dependent activated space inward to combine with the primary activated space, leaving a compression of space near the primary gestured form and an open expanse projected out from the secondary gestured form. (Fig. 27) The second original condition divided the three activated spaces equally in relation to the backdrop established by the primary gestured form, in the upper right corner of the contextual plane. (Fig. 28) The third original condition creates a serpentine spatial arrangement, where the three gestured forms organize themselves in a descending hierarchy of influence on their related activated spaces, while maintaining a balance of activated spaces. (Fig. 29) After examination of the three original conditions, a visual assessment was made on their spatial character and effectiveness to activate space. The first original condition was determined to be the least effective in character and activation. The second original condition was determined to be the most effective upon initial examination, however after further study and time-lapse sedimentation, it was found to have a larger temporary impact which fades over extended exposure and familiarity. The third original condition was determined to be the most effective after a study of extended duration, giving way to long term perceptual senses and memory. Therefore, for this study the third original condition was selected to continue a study of adjustment and refinement of the activated spaces; beginning with three variations of this original condition for improvement comparison.

The first variation from the original condition, was the shift of a balanced condition of the three spaces to a centralized dominance of the primary activated space defined by all three gestured forms, around the primary activated space's perimeter. (Fig. 29 and 30) To accomplish this shift, all three gestured forms were moved from the original condition; beginning with the primary gestured form, and a reactionary adjustment of the secondary and dependent gestured forms resulting from the primary gestured form's movement. The second variation from the original condition, kept the primary gestured form in the same location as the first variation; but moved the secondary form outward, opening up the dominate activated space. (Fig. 31 and 32) This resulted in a reactionary adjustment of the dependent gestured form, shifting the pointed end upward and reducing the dominate activated space. The third variation from the original condition, rotated the primary and secondary gestured forms slightly to the right of the second variation, resulting in a centering of the dominate activated space. (Fig. 33 and 34) In reaction to this, the dependent gestured form shifted upward into the dominate activated space, creating more attention to the activated space in the lower left corner of the contextual plane. The three variations to the original condition developed as a series, each variation growing out of the previous variation. Because of this, each variation can be viewed as improvements of the earlier condition; while still maintaining the initial character of the original condition, for relational identity and comparative ability of the two conditions. Through this process, there is a noticeable transformation in the variations; the first variation as a large departure from the original condition (Fig. 29 and 30); the second variation (Fig. 32) transforming from the first variation (Fig. 30), while regressing back toward the original condition (Fig. 29); and the third variation (Fig. 34) transforming from the second variation (Fig. 32), while still approaching even closer to the original condition. (Fig. 29).   By the time the variation process is complete, the third variation nears so closely to the original condition, that the original condition can be viewed as a developed transformation of the third variation. (Fig. 33 and 34)   The advantage to a series of variations such as this (in which an original condition is retained in the memory, as variations of a series are developed as extensions to each other), is to arrive at an improved condition (the third variation) of the original condition without directly comparing each adjustment and refinement to the foundational framework (the original condition).   Therefore, indirectly, the third variation (Fig. 34) is found to be an improved condition of the original condition (Fig. 29), to be used for further adjustments and refinements.

From the improved condition (the third variation of the original condition), an improvement is made with the slight movement of the secondary and dependent gestured forms in a counter clockwise rotation; making the definition of the three activated spaces clearer and more dynamic. (Fig. 35 and 36)   This adjustment is viewed as another improved condition, establishing a new condition from which further adjustments and refinements can be made. The series of three variations can be seen as a transformation of character from an asymmetrically dominate activated space (in the center of the contextual plane) with an implied directionality of a left- sided density to a right-sided tapering (Fig. 30); to a symmetrically compressed centralized balance of two smaller activated spaces (Fig. 34), nearing the original condition (Fig. 29).   However, with the latest improved condition (Fig. 36), the character can be seen to begin to split away from the symmetrically compressed centralized balance and regaining some of the first variation's asymmetrical directionality (Fig. 30), while dividing the lower left corner activated space from the previously dominate central activated space. (Fig. 35 and 36)   In short, the three variations made a move toward a single solidified character shifting to the right (echoing the original condition), while the recent improved condition maintains that development and is still able to break away a smaller independent activated space toward the lower left.

From the more recent improved condition (Fig. 36), several new variations develop making adjustments and refinements to the character's effectiveness in activating space.   The first variation from the improved condition, involves the concentration of influence from the secondary and dependent gestured forms onto a single activated space in the lower left corner of the contextual plane. (Fig. 37 and 38)   This results in the shift of the dominate activated space from the previous primary space to the lower left secondary and dependent space; thereby destroying the subtle distinguishing qualities of the initial character and eliminating any possibility of being considered as an improvement.   The second variation from the improved condition, shifts the pointed end of the dependent gestured figure downward slightly; to make a subtle enlargement of the primary activated space, establishing a balance between the primary and secondary activated spaces. (Fig. 39 and 40)   This movement enhances the character of the condition, however the secondary gestured form feels a little tight at the perimeter as a result of these two activated spaces creating more focused attention.   Therefore, with the third variation of the improved condition, the secondary gestured form shifts outward from the two activated spaces, creating a much larger and open contextual plane defined by the three perimeter gestured forms. (Fig. 41 and 42)   In doing this, the smaller activated space in the upper left corner of the contextual plane becomes minimized, and is in need of an enhanced definition to compete with the other two more dominate activated spaces.   To accomplish that, the forth variation of the improved condition, pulls the primary gestured form to the left, reducing the primary activated space's dominance.   This results in a reactionary counter clockwise rotation of the dependent gestured form, balancing the lower left activated space with the newly reduced primary activated space; reaching an equally shared enhancement and balancing point of the three gestured forms and three activated spaces. (Fig. 43 and 44)   The result of this forth variation is another (third) improved condition, from the previous (second) improved condition; drawing closer and closer to the desired unified condition.

The two series of conditions: the three variations from the original condition and the four variations from the improved condition, are given to illustrate the various approaches available in the adjustment and refinement of gestured forms and activated spaces.   The three variations of the original condition serve to demonstrate the advantages of an indirect form of visual analysis and familial sedimentation.   In contrast, the four variations of the improved condition serve to demonstrate the advantages of a more direct and continuous referral to a foundational framework (the improved condition), as a form of visual analysis and familial sedimentation.   Intermediate adjustments and subtle refinements were removed to simplify and clarify the explanation of the design process under study.   It is important to point out that the variations and improvements found here, in relation to each other, are not a true reflection of the subtlety in the adjustments studied, but were selected as only a partial documentation of the entire evolution or the resulting unified condition.

FIGURE 27: FIRST ORIGINAL CONDITION

Three defined spaces between and around the three gestured forms. The dependent activated space is turned inward to combine with the primary activated space, leaving a compression of space near the primary gestured form and an open expanse projected out from the secondary gestured form.

FIGURE 28: SECOND ORIGINAL CONDITION

Three defined spaces between and around the three gestured forms. The three activated spaces are divided equally in relation to the backdrop established by the primary gestured form, in the upper right corner of the contextual plane. As a result, the primary gestured form becomes static while the spaces are dynamic.

FIGURE 29: ORIGINAL CONDITION

THIRD ORIGINAL CONDITION: A serpentine spatial arrangement, where the three gestured forms organize themselves in a descending hierarchy of influence on their related activated spaces, while maintaining a balance of activated spaces. This condition, of the three, has the most enhancement of activated spaces.

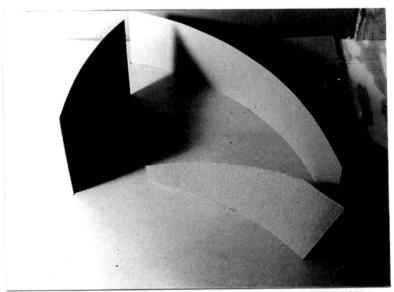

FIGURE 30: FIRST VARIATION FROM ORIGINAL CONDITION

The shift of a balanced condition of the three activated spaces to a centralized dominance of the primary activated space defined by all three gestured forms, around the primary activated space's perimeter. All three gestured forms are moved from the original condition; starting with the primary and the others reacting.

FIGURE 31: ORIGINAL CONDITION

A serpentine spatial arrangement, where the three gestured forms organize themselves in a descending hierarchy of influence on their related activated spaces, while maintaining a balance of activated spaces. A symmetrically compressed centralized dominate activated space, balanced with gestured forms and other spaces.

FIGURE 32: SECOND VARIATION FROM ORIGINAL CONDITION

The primary gestured form remains in the same location as in the first variation; but the secondary gestured form is moved outward, opening up the dominate activated space. This results in a reactionary adjustment of the dependent gestured form, shifting the pointed end upward and reducing the dominate activated space.

FIGURE 33: ORIGINAL CONDITION

A serpentine spatial arrangement, where the three gestured forms organize themselves in a descending hierarchy of influence on their related activated spaces, while maintaining a balance of activated spaces. A symmetrically compressed centralized dominate activated space, balanced with gestured forms and other spaces.

FIGURE 34: IMPROVED CONDITION

THIRD VARIATION FROM ORIGINAL CONDITION: The primary and secondary gestured forms are rotated slightly to the right of the second variation, resulting in a centering of the dominate activated space. In reaction, the dependent gestured form shifts upward drawing more attention to the lower left activated space.

FIGURE 35: IMPROVED CONDITION

The primary and secondary gestured forms are rotated slightly to the right of the second variation, resulting in a centering of the dominate activated space. In reaction, the dependent gestured form shifts upward into the dominate activated space, drawing more attention to the lower left activated space.

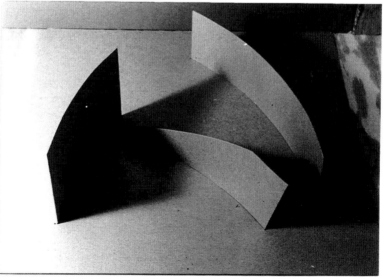

FIGURE 36: SECOND IMPROVED CONDITION

SECOND IMPROVED CONDITION FROM PREVIOUS IMPROVED CONDITION: The secondary and dependent gestured forms are moved from the third variation, in a slightly counter clockwise rotation making the definition of the three activated spaces clearer and more dynamic.

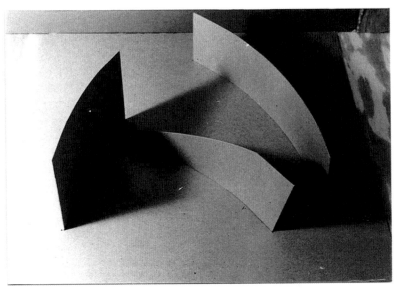

FIGURE 37: SECOND IMPROVED CONDITION

The lower left activated space splits away from the symmetrically compressed centralized balance of two dominate activated spaces (in the third variation: previous improved condition); and regains some of the first variation's asymmetrical directionality. In contrast to original condition, two dominate spaces are balanced.

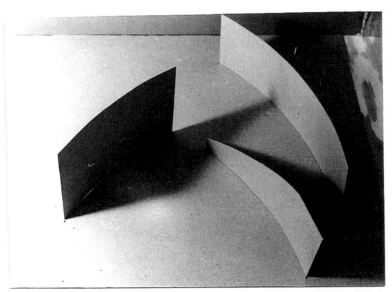

FIGURE 38: FIRST VARIATION FROM SECOND IMPROVED CONDITION

The secondary and dependent gestured forms concentrate their influence onto a single activated space in the lower left corner of the contextual plane. This results in a shift of the dominate activated space from the previous primary activated space to the lower left secondary and dependent activated space.

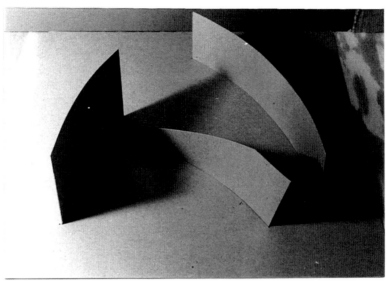

FIGURE 39: SECOND IMPROVED CONDITION

The lower left activated space splits away from the symmetrically compressed centralized balance of two dominate activated spaces (in the third variation: previous improved condition); and regains some of the first variation's asymmetrical directionality. In contrast to original condition, two dominate spaces are balanced.

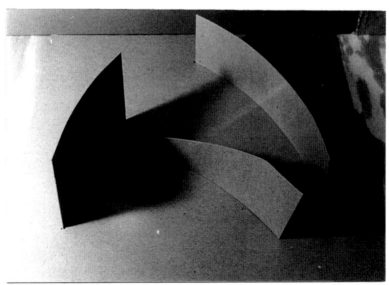

FIGURE 40: SECOND VARIATION FROM SECOND IMPROVED CONDITION

The pointed end of the dependent gestured form, shifts downward slightly to make a subtle enlargement of the primary activated space, establishing a balance between the primary and secondary activated spaces. The secondary gestured form feels a little tight as a result of the two spaces creating more focused attention.

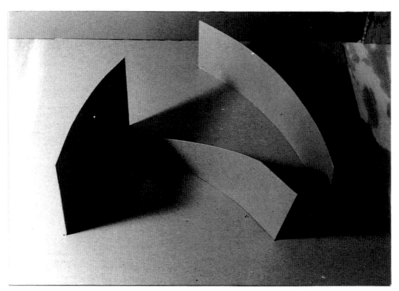

FIGURE 41: SECOND IMPROVED CONDITION

The lower left activated space splits away from the symmetrically compressed centralized balance of two dominate activated spaces (in the third variation: previous improved condition); and regains some of the first variation's asymmetrical directionality. In contrast to original condition, two dominate spaces are balanced.

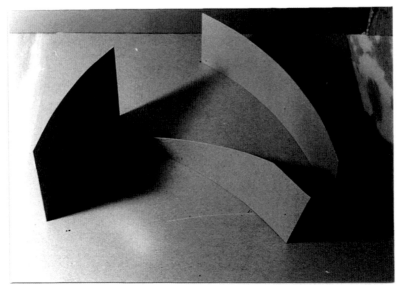

FIGURE 42: THIRD VARIATION FROM SECOND IMPROVED CONDITION

The secondary gestured form shifts outward from the two activated spaces, creating a much larger and open contextual plane defined by the three perimeter gestured forms. The smaller activated space in the upper left becomes minimized and is in need of an enhanced definition to compete with other two more dominate spaces.

FIGURE 43: SECOND IMPROVED CONDITION

The lower left activated space splits away from the symmetrically compressed centralized balance of two dominate activated spaces (in the third variation: previous improved condition); and regains some of the first variation's asymmetrical directionality. In contrast to original condition, two dominate spaces are balanced.

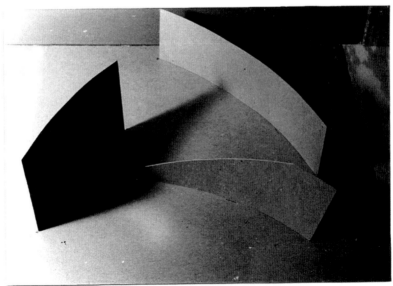

FIGURE 44: THIRD IMPROVED CONDITION

FORTH VARIATION FROM SECOND IMPROVED CONDITION: The primary gestured form moves left reducing the primary activated space's dominance. The dependent gestured form reacts in a counter clockwise rotation, balancing the lower left activated space with the newly reduced primary activated space.

REFERENCE LIST:

Acking, C. A. **Factorial Analysis of the Perception of an Interior.** (Architectural Psychology Conference) RIBA Publications, London, England, 1971.

Alexander, Christopher. **Notes on the Synthesis of Form.** Harvard University Press, Boston, Massachusetts, 1964.

Alexander, Christopher. **A Pattern Language: Towns, Buildings, Construction.** Oxford University Press, New York, New York, 1977.

Alp, Ahmet Vefik. **An Experimental Study of Aesthetic Response to Geometric Configurations of Architectural Space.** (Leonardo) The MIT Press, Cambridge, Massachusetts, Vol.26 No.2 1993.

Antico, Julianne. **Frog in a Well.** (Forthcoming Book) 94.12.20 oo

Arnheim, Rudolf. **The Dynamics of Architectural Form.** University of California Press, Berkeley and Los Angeles, California, 1977.

Barker, Roger G. **Ecological Psychology.** Stanford University Press, Stanford, California, 1968.

Barker, Roger G. **The Stream of Behavior.** Appleton Press, New York, New York, 1963.

Benedict, Ruth. **Patterns of Culture: An Analysis of Our Social Structure as Related to Primitive Civilizations.** Penguin Books Publishers, New York, New York, 1946.

Brittell, D. **The Connotative Meaning of the Architectural Form.** University of Illinois Press, Chicago, Illinois, 1969.

Burke, Edmund**. A Philosophical Enquiry into the Origin of our Ideas of the Sublime and Beautiful.** University of Notre Dame Press, Notre Dame, Indiana, 1986.

Burkhardt, Dieter. **Mowenbeobachtungen in Basel: First Description of Human Distances: Proxemics.** (Der Ornithalogische Beobachter) Vol.5 1944.

Canter, David. **Empirical Research in Environmental Psychology.** (Bulletin of the British Psychology Society) London, England, January 1974.

Canter, David. **Psychology for Architects.** Halsted Press, New York, New York, 1974.

Collins, John B. **Perceptual Dimensions of Architectural Space Validated against Behavioral Criteria.** University of Utah Press, Salt Lake City, Utah, 1969.

Colomina, Beatriz. **Sexuality and Space.** Princeton Architectural Press, New York, New York, 1992.

Craik, K. H. **The Comprehension of the Everyday Physical Environment.** (Journal of the American Institute of Planners) American Institute of Planners Publishers, Baltimore, Maryland, Vol.34 1968.

Craik, K. H. **Environmental Psychology.** (New Directions in Psychology) Holt, Rinehart and Winston publishers, New York, New York, 1970.

Crick, Francis. <u>**The Astonishing Hypothesis: The Scientific Search for the Soul.**</u> Charles Scribner's Sons Publishers, New York, New York, 1994.

Deleuze, Gilles. **The Fold: Leibniz and the Baroque.** (Architectural Design: Folding in Architecture) Academy Group Ltd., London, England, Profile No.102 1993.

Downs, R. M. and Stea, D. **Image and Environment: Cognitive Mapping and Spatial Behavior.** Aldine Press, Chicago, Illinois, 1973.

Eisenman, Peter. **The Affects of Singularity.** (Architectural Design: Theory and Experimentation) Academy Group Ltd., London, England, Profile No.100 1992.

Eisenman, Peter. **The Futility of Objects: Decomposition and the Processes of Difference.** (Article Manuscript) 12 / 27 / 82.

Endell, August. **The Beauty of Form and Decorative Art.** (Article published in Dekorative Kunst) Munich, Germany, 1898.

Esser, A. H. **Behavior and Environment: Use of Space by Animals and Man.** Plenum Press, New York, New York, 1971.

Freud, Sigmund. **Civilizations and Its Discontents.** Hogarth Press, London, England, 1930.

Garner, W. R. **Uncertainty and Structure as Psychological Concepts.** John Wiley and Sons Publishers, New York, New York, 1962.

Gibson, J. J. **The Senses Considered as Perceptual Systems.** Houghton Mifflin Press, Boston, Massachusetts, 1966.

Good, L. R., Spegel, S. M., and Bay, A. P. **Therapy by Design: Implications of Architecture for Human Behavior.** Charles C. Thomas Publishers, Springfield, Illinois, 1965.

Goodall, Jane. **In the Shadow of Man.** Houghton Mifflin Company, Boston, Massachusetts, 1971.

Grauman, Brigid. **On The Town.** (Passport Sabena) Ackroyd Publications, Brussels, Belgium, June 1994.

Greene, Herb. **Mind and Image: An Essay an Art and Architecture.** The University Press of Kentucky, Lexington, Kentucky, 1976.

Griffin, Donald R. **Animal Engineering.** (Scientific American) W. H. Freeman and Company, San Francisco, California, 1974.

Griffin, Donald R. <u>**Animal Minds.**</u> University of Chicago Press, Chicago, Illinois, 1992.

Groves, Philip M. and Rebec, George V. **Introduction to Biological Psychology,** 4th ed. William C. Brown Publishers, London, England, 1992.

Hall, Edward T.**Handbook for Proxemic Research**. Society for the Anthropology of Visual Communication, Washington, D. C., 1974.

Hall, Edward T. **The Hidden Dimension.** Doubleday Press, Garden City, New York, 1966.

Hall, Edward T. **Proxemics, the Study of Man's Spatial Relations.** (Man's Image in Medicine and Anthropology) Harvard University Press, Boston, Massachusetts, 1962.

Hay, D. R. **On the Science of those Proportions by which the Human Head and Countenance as Represented in Works of Ancient Greek Art are Distinguished from those of Ordinary Nature.** William Blackwood and Sons, London, England, 1849.

Hay, D. R. **Proportion, or the Geometric Principle of Beauty, Analyzed.** William Blackwood and Sons, London, England, 1843.

Heider, Fritz. **On Perception, Event Structure, and Psychological Environment.** (Psychological Issues) International Universities Press, New York, New York, Vol.1 No.3 1959.

Heider, R. and Simmel, M. **An Experimental Study of Apparent Behavior.** (Journal of Psychology) The Journal Press, Provincetown, Massachusetts, 1944.

Heschong, Lisa. **Thermal Delight in Architecture.** The MIT Press, Cambridge, Massachusetts, 1990.

Hogarth, William. **The Analysis of Beauty.** Oxford University Press, London, England, 1753.

Howard, H. E. **Territory in Bird Life.** Murray Publishers, London, England, 1920.

Howard, H. Seymour Jr. **Useful Curves and Curved Surfaces.** (Architectural Record) F. W. Dodge Corporation, New York, New York, August 1955 - February 1959.

Hutt, S. J. and Hutt, C. H. **Direct Observation and Measurement of Behavior.** Charles C. Thomas Publishers, Springfield, Illinois, 1970.

Ittelson, William H., Rivlin, Leanne G., and Proshansky, Harold M. **The Use of Behavioral Maps in Environmental Psychology.** (Environmental Psychology: Man and his Physical Setting) Holt, Rinehart and Winston Publishers, New York, New York, 1970.

Ittelson, William H. and Proshansky, Harold M. **An Introduction to Environmental Psychology: Research Methods in Environmental Psychology.** Holt, Rinehart and Winston Publishers, New York, New York, 1974.

Johnson, Susan and Marano, Hara Estroff. Attachment: **The Immutable Longing for Contact.** (Psychology Today) Sussex Publishers, New York, New York, Vol.27 No.2 1994.

Kant, Immanuel. **Observations on the Feeling of the Beautiful and Sublime.** University of California Press, Berkeley, California, 1965.

Kipnis, Jeffrey. **Of Objectology.** (Pratt Journal of Architecture) Rizzoli Books, New York, New York, Spring 1988.

Kipnis, Jeffrey. **Post-Analytic Space.** (Studio Lecture Abstract) The Ohio State University, School of Architecture, Columbus, Ohio, 1990.

Kipnis, Jeffrey. **Towards a New Architecture.** (Architectural Design: Folding in Architecture) Academy Group Ltd., London, England, Profile No.102 1993.

Koffka, Kurt. **The Growth of the Mind:** An Introduction to Child-Psychology. Harcourt, Brace & World, Inc., New York, New York, 1924.

Koffka, Kurt. **Principles of Gestalt Psychology.** Harcourt, Brace & World, Inc., New York, New York, 1935.

Krier, Robert. **Urban Space.** Rizzoli Books, New York, New York, 1979.

Kuspit, Donald B. **The Subjective Aspect of Critical Evaluation.** (Art Criticism) State University at Stony Brook, Stony Brook, New York, No.3 1987.

Kuspit, Donald B. **Clement Greenberg: Art Critic.** The University of Wisconsin Press, Madison, Wisconsin, 1979.

Lang, Jon. **Creating Architectural Theory: The Role of the Behavioral Sciences in Environmental Design.** Van Nostrand Reinhold Company, New York, New York, 1987.

Laubin, Reginald and Gladys. **The Indian Tipi: its history, construction, and use**, 2nd ed. University of Oklahoma Press, Norman, Oklahoma, 1989.

Lewin, Kurt. **Field Theory in Social Science.** Harper Publishers, Inc., New York, New York, 1951.

Lewin, Kurt. **Principle of Topological Psychology**. McGraw-Hill Publishers, New York, New York, 1936.

Lobell, John. **Architecture and the Structures of Consciousness.** (Pratt Journal of Architecture) Rizzoli Books, New York, New York, Spring 1988.

Lowenthal, D. **Environmental Perception and Behavior.** University of Chicago Press, Chicago, Illinois, 1967.

Luria, S. M., Kinney, J. S., and Weissman, S. **Distance Estimates with 'filled' and 'unfilled' Space.** (Perceptual and Motor Skills) Southern Universities Press, Missoula, Montana, Vol.24 1967.

Lym, Glenn Robert. **A Psychology of Building: How We Shape and Experience Our Structured Spaces.** Prentice-Hall Press, Englewood Cliffs, New Jersey, 1980.

Lynn, Greg. **Architectural Curvilinearity: the Folded, the Pliant, and the Supple.** (Architectural Design: Folding in Architecture) Academy Group Ltd., London, England, Profile No.102 1993.

Maslow, A. H. and Mintz, N. L. **Effects of Aesthetic Surroundings.** (Journal of Psychology) The Journal Press, Provincetown, Massachusetts, 1956.

Michotte, A. E. **The Emotional Significance of Movement.** Penguin Books, Baltimore, Maryland, 1968.

Missel, Renee and Foster, Jodie. **Nell.** (Based on the play 'Idioglossia' by Mark Handley) Twentieth Century Fox, An Egg Pictures Production, New York, New York, 1994.

Muthesius, Hermann. <u>**Wo stehen wir?**</u> (Speech given at the Werkbund Congress: cited and translated by Banham) Cologne, Germany, 1911.

Pearson, David. **Making Sense of Architecture.** (Architectural Review) MBC Architectural Press & Building Publications, London, England, October 1991.

Perez-Gomez, Alberto. **Architecture and the Crisis of Modern Science.** The MIT Press, Cambridge, Massachusetts, 1983.

Piedmont-Palladino, Susan C. **The America's Cup: A Design Parable.** (The Journal of Architectural Education) Association of Collegiate Schools of Architecture, Washington, D. C., May 1993.

Rapoport, Amos. **History and Precedent in Environmental Design.** University of Wisconsin-Milwaukee, Plenum Press, Milwaukee, Wisconsin, 1990.

Rapoport, Amos. **On the Cultural Responsiveness of Architecture.** (Journal of Architectural Education) Association of Collegiate Schools of Architecture, Washington, D. C., Fall 1987.

Robbins, M. C. **Perceptual Environments and Pattern Preferences.** (Perceptual and Motor Skills) Southern Universities Press, Missoula, Montana, Vol.26 1968.

Sanoff, H. **Experimental Studies of Physical Attributes of the Visual Environment.** (Architectural Psychology Newsletter) Autumn 1968.

Sanoff, H. **Measuring Attributes of the Visual Environment.** (Designing for Human Behavior) Dowden Press, Stroudsbourg, Pennsylvania, 1974.

Schaller, George. **The Serengeti Lion.** The University of Chicago Press, Chicago, Illinois, 1972.

Schlueb, Matthew Thomas. **gestured form and activated space.** (Graduate Thesis) Pratt Institute, Brooklyn, New York, Fall 1994.

Schlueb, Matthew Thomas. **Independent Study: Thesis Research.** (Industrial Design) Pratt Institute, Brooklyn, New York, Fall 1993.

Schlueb, Matthew Thomas. <u>**Mousetrap**</u>. (Short Story Manuscript) 93.3.18 oo

Schlueb, Matthew Thomas. **Undergraduate Thesis: thesis-work installation.** Pratt Institute, Brooklyn, New York, Spring 1994.

Searles, Harold F. **The Non-Human Environment in Normal Development and in Schizophrenia.** International Universities Press, New York, New York, 1960.

Sekuler, Robert and Blake, Randolph. **Perception**, 2nd ed. McGraw-Hill Publishers, New York, New York, 1990.

Shepard, R. N. **Analysis of Proximities: Multidimensional Scaling with an Unknown Distance Function**. (Psychometrika) Psychometric Society Publishers, Chicago, Illinois, Vol.27 1962.

Skalski, Martin. <u>**Theory of Design Mutation.**</u> (Car Styling 98) Car Styling Publishing, Tokyo, Japan, January 1994.1.

Sommer, Robert. **Personal Space: The Behavioral Basis of Design.** Prentice-Hall Publishers, Englewood Cliffs, New Jersey, 1969.

Sommer, Robert. **Social Design: Creating Buildings with People in Mind.** Prentice-Hall Publishers, Englewood Cliffs, New Jersey, 1983.

Sommer, Robert. <u>**Tight Spaces: Hard Architecture and How to Humanize It.**</u> Prentice-Hall Publishers, Englewood Cliffs, New Jersey, 1974.

Stea, David. **Space, Territory and Human Movements.** (Landscape 15) J. B. Jackson Publishers, Sante Fe, New Mexico, Autumn 1965.

Stokes, Adrian. **Inside Out: An Essay in the Psychology and Aesthetic Appeal of Space.** Faber and Faber Limited, London, England, 1947.

Thiel, P. **Notes on the Description, Scaling, Notation and Scoring of Some Perceptual and Cognitive Attributes of the Physical Environment**. (Environmental Psychology: Man and his Physical Setting) Holt, Rinehart and Winston Publishers, New York, New York, 1970.

Thiel, P. **Towards an Experiential Envirotecture**. (Article Manuscript) University of Washington Press, Seattle, Washington.

Wheeler, L. **Behavioral Slide Rule for College Architects**. (Interiors) Whitney Publications, New York, New York, Vol.127 No.5 December 1967.

Wilson, Colin St. John. **The Natural Imagination: An Essay on the Experience of Architecture**. (Architectural Review) MBC Architectural Press & Building Publications, London, England, January 1989.

Winkel, G. H. and Sasanoff, R. **An Approach to an Objective Analysis of Behavior in Architectural Space.** University of Washington Press, Seattle, Washington, 1966.

Wolhill, J. F. **Amount of Stimulus Exploration and Preference as Differential Functions of Stimulus Complexity.** (Perception and Psychology 4) Perception and Society Publishers, New York, New York, 1968.

Wollheim, Richard. **The Image in Form: Selected Writings of Adrian Stokes.** Harper & Row Publishers, New York, New York, 1972.

" Through purely logical thinking we can attain no knowledge,
whatsoever of the empirical world. "

Albert Einstein
[Gestalt Psychology]

When a jazz quintet is playing a riff, in a night club, there is an unspoken understanding between the musicians about the order and duration each is to play. This understanding is heard by those people who are able to listen.